T0207913

101
SUCCESS
SECRETS
for Gifted Kids

Second Edition

101
SUCCESS
SECRETS
for Gifted Kids

Advice, Quizzes, and Activities for Dealing With
Stress, Expectations, Friendships, and More

Christine Fonseca

Routledge
Taylor & Francis Group

First published in 2020 by Prufrock Press Inc.

Published 2021 by Routledge
605 Third Avenue, New York, NY 10017
2 Park Square, Milton Park, Abingdon, Oxon OX14 4RN

Routledge is an imprint of the Taylor & Francis Group, an informa business

Copyright © 2020 by Taylor & Francis Group

Cover and layout design by Allegra Denbo

All rights reserved. No part of this book may be reprinted or reproduced or utilised in any form or by any electronic, mechanical, or other means, now known or hereafter invented, including photocopying and recording, or in any information storage or retrieval system, without permission in writing from the publishers.

Notice:
Product or corporate names may be trademarks or registered trademarks, and are used only for identification and explanation without intent to infringe.

ISBN 13: 978-1-0321-4316-3 (hbk)
ISBN 13: 978-1-6463-2036-3 (pbk)

DOI: 10.4324/9781003232575

Dedication

For my mom, whose life was the example
of embracing one's giftedness.

Table of Contents

Acknowledgements

Every new book or edition is a unique journey. Writing this edition during the heart of a global pandemic was an interesting experience, and I'm so thankful for those who assisted me on this particular project:

To my partner, my husband, my soulmate— I am confident that I couldn't have written this without your continuing love and support. The original book was completed as my mother took her last breaths. This edition was completed as the world wrestled with a global pandemic. In both experiences, you were my strength when my emotions overwhelmed me. You helped with the household chores, provided space when I needed it, and enabled me, once again, to follow my passions. Thank you for all you are for the family and me.

To my amazing children, Fabiana and Erika—you were my original inspiration for this book. Your meanderings as gifted children provided so much of the content of this book. Thank you for living true to yourself and thriving as unicorns. You are inspirations to the world.

To Joel McIntosh, Katy McDowall, and the entire team at Prufrock Press—we have partnered on projects for more than a decade. Thank you for the continued collaboration. I am proud of all we have created together and all we may create in the future.

Finally, to the thousands of gifted and talented children, parents, and educators that have contributed to both editions of this book—your ideas and insights are highlighted throughout the pages of this book in the quotes and words. I am sincerely humbled by each and every one of you. Your stories and advice are a source of inspiration that extends far beyond the pages of this book.

Introduction

Why This Book

Being identified as gifted means a lot more than being smart. For most kids, it means being good in school, even though you get bored quickly. It may also mean that you can figure things out really fast—maybe even quicker than your parents or teachers. But, being bright also means feeling stressed out. A lot. Peers, the pressures of school, the expectations of parents, and the feeling that no one understands you are enough to make most kids wish that the label of giftedness never existed.

That's where this book comes in. *101 Success Secrets for Gifted Kids* is full of the tips kids need to understand and make the most out of the gifted label. Advice and ideas from thousands of kids just like you fill the pages, giving you everything you need to be a success—in school, at home, and in life.

 DOI: 10.4324/9781003232575-1

The second edition of *101 Success Secrets for Gifted Kids* begins with an overview of giftedness that covers what it means to have the gifted label, the characteristics of giftedness, and the emotional aspects of being a high-potential human.

The next three sections discuss specific problems that arise in your unique world, separated into the areas where you spend most of your time—school, home, and in the world. The book ends with a few additional resources, just in case you want more information.

How to Use This Book

This book was designed to be used as you need it. Read the section that relates to whatever it is you are going through at the time. Got a problem with school and perfectionism? Turn to that section. Want to know how to deal with your parents or siblings? Check out what others did. Friendship dilemmas? No problem—just refer to that section. Curious about multipotentiality and what it means for your future? Go to that part of the book. The point is to use the book as you need it and use it often. What makes sense today may change as you get older.

101 Success Secrets for Gifted Kids was also designed with your parents in mind. Even though they probably understand what you're going through, parents sometimes forget what it is to be young. This book can help them remember all of the issues that creep up in your world. Don't be afraid to share parts of this book with them or any other adult who needs a little help understanding what it is to be you.

And finally, if you find the book helpful and want to offer advice to kids like you, please email me at christine@christinefonseca.com. I'm always looking for great tips and more ways to help kids. Sharing your own experiences is an excellent way for you to give back to others. Your advice may even end up in the next edition of this book!

A Word to Parents and Educators

Growing up with a gifted label can be hard work. Typically blessed with highly intelligent and intuitive minds, gifted kids are confronted with intense emotions that change rapidly, leaving them feeling confused, frustrated, and alone. That's where this book comes in. Packed with advice and success secrets from other children, *101 Success Secrets for Gifted Kids* sheds light on the world of giftedness. By offering practical advice for kids from the ones they listen to the most—other kids—it is my hope that this book can be a resource for children, parents, and educators as they navigate through the sometimes treacherous waters of giftedness.

Use this book to address various concerns as they come up. Or, read it first and then share it with your children. Either way, be sure to talk about the information and advice with your kids. Use the ideas as a springboard to open the lines of communication. If you find something particularly helpful, shoot me a note at christine@christinefonseca.com and let me know.

I wish you much success in being the coach your children need as they progress through their years and embrace everything it means to be gifted.

WHAT IT MEANS TO BE GIFTED

Understanding how to live life as a gifted person begins with understanding what it means to be gifted in the first place. The next three chapters will cover everything you need to know about being gifted, from the attributes of giftedness and the problems that sometimes arise, to the crazy mixed-up feelings most gifted kids share, to cultivating your intensities as a source of strength for you throughout your life.

To get started, I've got a little quiz to test your knowledge of giftedness. Answer all five true/false questions before you read this section. Once you're done reading all three chapters, try the quiz again. Did anything change?

 DOI: 10.4324/9781003232575-2

Quiz: What Do I Know About Being Gifted?

Directions: Circle your answer for each question.

1. Being gifted means I should always earn good grades.

    true   *false*

2. If I make a lot of mistakes on my work at school, it means I can't possibly be gifted.

    true   *false*

3. Being super sensitive to things is not part of being gifted.

    true   *false*

4. Learning is always easy for gifted people.

    true   *false*

5. Giftedness only has to do with learning, not with how I feel about things.

    true   *false*

THINK DIFFERENT

So, you took a special test at school, your parents and teachers filled out a few forms, and now everyone says you're gifted. What on Earth does that mean? Will you get extra work now? Are people going to expect great things from you all of the time?

"Being gifted means I look at the world differently than some of my friends. It also means that some people are going to assume that I never have to work hard. The truth is I work really, really hard at things. And, I hate it when, after working so hard, I don't do well."—*Olivia, age 11*

Will you get to go on special field trips or participate in special activities? The questions are endless, and they come back to the same issue . . .

What does it mean to be gifted?

The truth is that there is not one agreed-upon answer as to what it means to be gifted. Organizations like the National Association for Gifted Children (NAGC) have tried to shed light on this by coming up with definitions for giftedness. NAGC (2019) said that a gifted person performs at higher levels

DOI: 10.4324/9781003232575-3

> "Being in GATE doesn't mean you're different from everyone else; it just means you think in different ways."—*Hiro, age 13*

than peers of the same age and experience. Yeah, I know. That doesn't really clear anything up, does it?

Researchers agree that there is a specific set of characteristics that define giftedness—smart, strong reasoning skills, and intellectually curious (Clark, 2013). Perfectionism, strong emotions, and high sensitivity to everything are also aspects of giftedness (Fonseca, 2016).

These characteristics still don't say what it *means* to be gifted or how giftedness impacts your world.

SUCCESS SECRET #1

Giftedness isn't something you can change. It's how your brain works.

Giftedness, like eye color or height, isn't something you can choose. It's how you're hardwired. Success at school—or in life—really has nothing to do with it.

Giftedness means that you are biologically wired to view the world in a certain way. That's what all of those characteristics listed above refer to—how you actually think about things. You can try to think in a different way, try not to be gifted. You can fail in school and try to blend in with your friends. Regardless, you will still be gifted. It isn't something you can change.

Table 1: My Gifted Brain lists some of the unique features of a gifted brain. All of these unique features impact how you think about the world. It's what makes you gifted and what makes you, you.

SUCCESS SECRET #2

Being gifted does not mean you are perfect at everything.

Yeah, I know. You think you should know everything if you're really gifted, right? Wrong. Being gifted has nothing to do with what you know. Not

TABLE 1
My Gifted Brain

Attribute	What It Means
Increased grey matter volume	You can learn and store more information.
Efficient white matter	The connections between the different areas of the brain work more efficiently.
Increased sensitivity to information from the environment	You are more sensitive to what you see, hear, feel, taste, etc.
Increased processing speed	Because of the grey matter and white matter, you process information quickly.
Increased emotional awareness	Because of the increased integration of your processing areas in the brain, you have enhanced emotional awareness.

Note. Adapted from Tetreault et al., 2016.

one thing. Giftedness is about how you view things, how you learn, and your capacity for performing at high levels.

It has nothing to do with being perfect. In fact, the truth is, no one is perfect at everything. So, relax a little, and realize that the label doesn't mean you are expected to be perfect, no matter what you think your parents and teachers want.

> "Don't get all stressed over the title 'gifted.' I did and I thought that it meant I had to get all A's and had to be perfect. I was wrong."—*Katie, age 12*

SUCCESS SECRET #3

Not all gifted kids are high achievers.

One of the more common myths that kids, parents, and even teachers may believe is that being gifted means you are supposed to get high grades all of the time (Webb et al., 2007). Not true at all. In fact, a lot of gifted kids struggle in school. It doesn't mean they aren't gifted, though. Usually, it just means they haven't figured out how to make school work for them—something we will talk about in the next section.

> "I hate that teachers always assume that since I have a GATE label, it must mean that I know all the answers. The truth is, there are a lot of things I don't know. And school is often really challenging for me."—*Rushon, age 12*

So, if you are struggling in a particular subject or even with school in general, don't assume that it means you aren't gifted. Everyone struggles from time to time.

SUCCESS SECRET #4

Learn everything you can about your giftedness.

Most of the things that make you unique involve the way you think about the world. Solving problems quickly and creatively, learning at a fast pace, and understanding difficult concepts are all things you do every day. Some of the other characteristics of how you think include being highly curious (which is why some gifted kids like to take things apart and figure out how they work), having a vivid imagination, and demonstrating an intense need to learn (even if you think school is boring).

Giftedness doesn't end with how you think. It involves how you act and behave as well. Gifted kids thrive when things are logical and hate it when everything seems chaotic. They often understand the complex problems that exist in the world and hate it when adults underestimate them. And, gifted kids think that perfection is required—so much so that they often decide not to try something for fear of failing (Fonseca, 2016). Review Table 2: My Gifted Attributes and see how many of these common attributes of giftedness you demonstrate.

> "Being gifted doesn't really change who you are. It just changes what you know about who you are."—*Becca, age 14*

SUCCESS SECRET #5

Your gifted brain can lie to you.

Guess what? All of those feelings about being perfect—sometimes they are wrong. Sometimes your brain can lie to you and make you believe some-

TABLE 2
My Gifted Attributes

Intellectual Attributes	Personality Attributes	Social-Emotional Attributes
▪ Exceptional reasoning ability ▪ Intellectual curiosity ▪ Rapid learning rate ▪ Facility with abstracts ▪ Complex thought processes ▪ Vivid imagination ▪ Early moral concern ▪ Passion for learning	▪ Insightful ▪ Need to understand ▪ Need for mental stimulation ▪ Perfectionism ▪ Need for precision or logic ▪ Excellent sense of humor ▪ Sensitivity/Empathy ▪ Intensity	▪ High performance standards ▪ Internal motivation ▪ Moral maturity ▪ Resiliency ▪ Self-actualization ▪ Empathy ▪ Emotional intensity

thing that just isn't true. It happens because gifted kids think quickly, linking together ideas fast—often, too fast. Sometimes two wrong ideas get linked, and gifted kids begin to believe things that may not be true. For example, a gifted kid may link together the idea that gifted kids are good at everything they try and the idea that not being good at something means you are not gifted. When these are linked, the gifted student may feel too much pressure to be perfect, believing that anything less means the gifted label was a lie.

So, what's a gifted kid to do? Slow the process down, and learn to discern what is correct and accurate versus what is not. Learning to tell the difference between when your brain is lying to you and when it is not is critically important to managing the natural intensities your giftedness can bring.

An easy strategy to use when discerning whether or not your brain is correct in its assumption is a technique I call PROOF (see "Tips for Using the PROOF Technique"). In this method, you are literally looking for proof that what you believe is true. For example, let's pretend your brain says, "I am horrible at math. I will never learn it. So I must NOT be smart." Use the PROOF method to look for evidence that you are, in fact, horrible at math. You will also need to prove that being horrible at math means you are not smart. Evaluate your math grades over time, look at test scores, and talk with your teachers and parents. Odds are good you are not horrible at math at all. It's more likely that you are just struggling with a particular concept. Even if you do discover that math is not your best subject, it doesn't mean you are

Tips for Using the PROOF Technique

1. What message is your brain telling you? Be specific.

2. How do you know it's the correct message? What proof can you find that it is true?

3. If you find that the message is true, what can you do about it?

4. If you find that the message is untrue, what is the correct message?

5. How can you train your brain to stop giving you false messages?

not smart. Do you have strong abilities in other areas? Do you demonstrate other characteristics of giftedness? That could be your proof that being bad at math does not mean you are dumb. It just means you will have to work harder in math than in your other subjects.

SUCCESS SECRET **#6**

There are many ways to learn information.

Part of understanding yourself and reaching your potential involves understanding how you best learn information. Do you prefer to listen to your teachers? Are you visual, seeing words as pictures in your head? Are you more hands-on, preferring to touch and manipulate things as a way to learn? Take the short quiz "How Do You Learn?" to help determine your primary way of learning. Use this information to help you make the most of your school experiences.

Go through and look at your answers. True on numbers 1, 4, and 7 means you learn best by seeing things. True on 2, 5, and 8 means you need to use your hands and touch things to learn best. And true on 3, 6, and 9 means listening to information is your best way of learning. Some of you will find that you answered true to questions for each of the areas. This means you are a multimodal learner.

There are lots of other ways to learn and lots of other tools to discover your learning strengths. The important thing is to begin to understand how you learn best.

Quiz: How Do You Learn?

Directions: Circle your answer for each question.

1. I learn best when I can see a picture of something.

   true   false

2. I like to build things.

   true   false

3. I talk a lot about my day and really like to listen to other people talking.

   true   false

4. When my teacher is talking, I make pictures of the words in my head—it makes remembering things easier.

   true   false

5. If I write things down, I remember them better—even when I don't study.

   true   false

6. I understand a story that I hear better than a story that I read.

   true   false

7. When I study vocabulary words, I like to make a picture of the word or concept. It helps me remember them better.

   true   false

8. Using blocks for math and sentence strips for writing really helps me remember things.

   true   false

9. I spell words out loud when I am studying—that way I remember them better.

   true   false

SUCCESS SECRET **#7**

Learning new information does not mean you are dumb.

I remember when my oldest daughter was starting third grade. She was so angry with me for not teaching her everything she needed to learn before the year started. She hated learning new things at school. She always felt like she should already know everything. When she realized she didn't know it all, she would get frustrated.

I bet you feel that way at times, too. It's one of those things related to being gifted—the feeling that if you are really as smart as everyone thinks you are, you should already know everything about everything.

> "I get very frustrated when I don't understand something I'm being taught for the first time, even though I know it's okay not to understand some things."—*Maya, age 14*

In your mind, you know this isn't true. But, in your heart, you can't help it—you really feel like learning new things means you're not smart. It's hard to change that belief, it really is, but remember this: Remaining open to learning new things is one of the smartest things you will ever do in your life. It will enable you to make new discoveries about yourself, the subjects you are studying, and even the world. So try to stay as open-minded as you can . . . and when that little voice in your head tries to convince you that you should already know everything, learn to replace the thoughts with something more accurate—learning something new is the best way to grow your brain.

SUCCESS SECRET **#8**

Stay open to new ideas.

As I mentioned in the previous success secret, learning new things is important for your brain. By stretching your intellectual and creative muscles, you allow yourself the freedom of seeing things in a unique way. This, in turn, enables you to understand the different points of view present in any situation. Why does this matter?

Taking a fresh perspective not only helps develop your skills of empathy and compassion (essential pieces of emotional intelligence that we'll talk about later), but also helps improve your problem-solving skills and abstract thinking. By seeing the world from a different point of view, you can begin to understand why things are the way they are and why people do the things they do. You may begin to see new and innovative ways to solve difficult problems, both those that concern learning and those that concern relationships.

Check out the "Tips for Taking a Fresh Perspective." Learning to view the world from new or varied perspectives is a great way to broaden your worldview and deepen your understanding of others.

SUCCESS SECRET **#9**

Identify and use your character strengths.

In addition to the different aspects of giftedness already discussed, it is important to learn about your character strengths. These are aspects of your personality, like kindness, hope, love of learning, and a strong sense of justice. Researchers have discovered that identifying and using your character strengths can result in more happiness and greater life fulfillment (Baumann et al., 2019). Furthermore, specifically looking for ways you live your strengths and spotting other people's strengths can increase resilience and emotional intelligence (Niemiec, 2019).

Take some time to get to know your strengths. You can use tools like the free strengths survey from Thrively (https://www.thrively.com/student) or the character strengths survey from the VIA Institute on Character (https://www.viacharacter.org/survey/account/register). Of course, be sure to get parent permission before completing any online survey.

Once you have determined your character strengths, take time to recognize when you might be using your strengths. This may be difficult initially. Most people struggle to see their strengths. If you are having a hard time, start by looking for your friends and family's strengths. That may make it easier to begin to recognize your own strengths. The "Tips for Developing Your Strengths" may help.

Tips for Taking a Fresh Perspective

1. Imagine you are a character in a book. Try to feel what they must have felt during one scene of the story.

2. Pick a favorite fairy tale and rewrite the story from a minor character's perspective. For example, rewrite Goldilocks from the point of view of the mother bear or maybe even from the little chair's point of view. How are things different?

3. With a parent's help, stand on top of a chair or the bed. Does the room look different from that view? How?

4. Go with your parents on a drive into the mountains. How do things look different from the peak of the mountains compared to the bottom or the middle? If you don't live near mountains, try imagining this same task from a tall building or monument. For example, does the Lincoln Memorial look different as you move further up the stairs?

5. Draw a picture of your backyard from three points of view:
    a. Sitting in your house and looking outside
    b. Being a bird and flying overhead
    c. Being a small bug and crawling across it

Looking at the world from a fresh perspective is a great way to learn to broaden your views on everything.

SUCCESS SECRET **#10**

Grow your gifts and talents.

Throughout this chapter, you've learned what it means to have a gifted brain. You've also learned that it is important to remember that being gifted isn't an all-or-nothing thing. You can—and should—strive to grow your gifts and talents throughout your lifetime. Take a talented writer or artist. Without the hours of practice on their craft, they would not be successful in their respective fields, no matter how strong their natural gifts. This is also true for you. Put the time in to understand your giftedness, develop your talents, and grow as a human. This will only make your gifts that much stronger.

Tips for Developing Your Strengths

Try these strategies to help you recognize and develop your different character strengths.

1. **Seeking Strengths**: Look for strengths in others and yourself. When you see one, call it out; everyone likes to hear about their strengths.

2. **Strengths Innovation**: Use your strengths in new ways. Commit to one new way per week.

3. **Strength-Based Problem-Solving**: Use your strengths to overcome life's difficulties. Actively seek ways to use your strengths when you are challenged.

Note. Adapted from Fonseca, 2019.

Take a few moments to reflect on your many talents and gifted attributes and then complete the worksheet "Growing My Gifts and Talents." Use the worksheet as a guide for being a lifelong learner and continually building your life.

Parents Sound Off

Parents have their own ideas of giftedness. Reading their thoughts may help you refine your beliefs.

- "Gifted is something I identify as exceptional—like an artist who has a natural ability to sketch."—*Devi*
- "Gifted means you learn in a different way from other students. It also means being bored in school, getting distracted due to being bored, and struggling socially."—*Julie*
- "Giftedness means nothing other than specialized instruction in the younger grades. At least, that is how it seems in most cases."—*Linda*
- "Giftedness means not just learning at a faster rate than other kids, but being intense on a very fundamental level."—*Andie*

WORKSHEET
Growing My Gifts and Talents

Directions: Write a list of your giftedness attributes. Add your talents to the list. Then complete the rest of the worksheet. Use the example as a guide.

List of Gifts and Talents	Something I'd Like to Improve	Ideas of How I Can Improve That Area
Very fast at learning math	*I'd like to master two-digit multiplication before the end of the semester.*	*Practice more of these kinds of problems. Learn tricks to do this quickly.*

- "I used to think giftedness had to do with more challenging school work. And then I had a gifted child. Wow, gifted is so much more than being smart."—*Jamie*

Yes, parents are sometimes as confused as you are over what it all means. But, confused or not, they do understand that giftedness is more than getting good grades in school.

Overall, the definition of giftedness is elusive. There are myths that cloud people's thinking and misinformation that can work against you. Your job is to learn everything you can about the attributes of giftedness, and then figure out how to make things work for you. Learning how to get your needs met through the educational system, as well as the support you need from friends and family, is a life skill that will help you now and in the future.

What Do You Think?

Now it's your turn. Take a few moments and ask yourself the following questions. See how you feel about the label and all that is good—and bad—about being gifted.

What does being gifted mean to you?

What is the best part about being gifted? The worst?

What advice would you share with those younger than you about being gifted?

Chapter

2

FEEL DIFFERENT

Now you know that being gifted isn't just about being smart. It's how you're hardwired. Your giftedness influences how you view and interact with the world. And it influences your emotions—those crazy, mixed-up ways you may feel about . . . well . . . everything.

Intense feelings are a normal part of giftedness. Unfortunately, intense emotions seldom garner a lot of respect from your peers, family, or teachers. Many times the reactions of others may cause you to feel ashamed of your strong emotions, like there is something wrong with you. The truth is that emotional intensity is just part of what it means to be gifted.

But what is emotional intensity, exactly?

> "I stress if I don't get A's on everything, I get really emotional with my friends, and I struggle with some of my school stuff. But, it is who I am."—*Song, age 9*

     DOI: 10.4324/9781003232575-4

Super happy and super sad feelings are part of it. So are the rapid changes in your emotions. And it is so much more: Emotional intensity can be expressed physically, through headaches, stomachaches, heart palpations, and even the need to constantly be moving. It can also be expressed as fear, anxiety, guilt, and shame. Usually it refers to a combination of all of those things occurring together (Fonseca, 2016; Sword, 2006a).

Emotional intensity isn't a bad thing, despite how bad some of the descriptions may sound. Intensity is actually just the way you view the world—through bold thoughts and feelings, as opposed to the more sedated ways your friends may view things.

SUCCESS SECRET **#11**

Giftedness and intense emotions go hand in hand.

Remember, giftedness involves your thoughts, actions, and feelings. It also involves the way in which these things interact with the world. For gifted kids, everything is more intense. This means that you think more deeply than other kids, you behave in a way that is more focused or intense, and you feel things at a deeper level. When you are happy, you are super happy. But, when you are sad, you are very sad. There is no middle ground—no half-way point with you (Fonseca, 2016).

> "All that emotional drama you start going through in fourth and fifth grade—don't freak out about it. It's normal. And the sooner you learn to manage it, the easier everything gets."—*Fiona, age 12*

This is not a bad thing, although sometimes it may feel like you are on an emotional rollercoaster that never seems to end.

SUCCESS SECRET **#12**

Your crazy, intense emotions are normal . . . and good.

As I've already mentioned, emotional intensity is a normal and natural part of being gifted. That doesn't mean that the way you react to your emotions works to help you. In fact, I bet you often react in ways that work against you. Like yelling when you're frustrated or crying when you get overwhelmed. You

> "Learn to embrace your emotions. Things got so much better when I started to embrace mine." —*Madison, age 14*

may even get stuck in your thoughts and feelings at times, constantly thinking about things that bother you and believing that you'll never be able to make yourself stop. These ways of reacting can bring out the worst parts of your normal emotional intensity and create an even bigger problem.

The first step in changing all of this is to recognize that feeling things intensely is not the problem. Not at all.

SUCCESS SECRET #13

The only thing you can really control is you.

Intensity can impact how you interact with your friends and family. You may find it hard to find friends. Perhaps you can't relate to the more typical things kids your age enjoy. For some gifted kids, the problem is really about not knowing how to connect with kids in general. Friendships are often a large source of frustration.

You may not understand why your friends get annoyed with you, or why the kids at school think you're bossy or mean. It can be really hard and make you feel very sad, but guess what?

You have no control over how the other kids act toward you. In fact, you really have no control over anyone else. The only thing you do have control over is you, your behavior, and your reactions. Although that may not seem like enough some days, it really is a very powerful thing. Remembering that you are the only thing you have control over can be hard. That's where the "Tips for the Hula Hoop Trick" come in.

Use this technique every time you find yourself trying to change how other people behave. It will help you remember that the only one you can really change is you.

Tips for the Hula Hoop Trick

1. Imagine there is a hula hoop on the ground.

2. Step into the middle of it.

3. Everything outside of the hula hoop you have no control over—this includes friends, family, school . . . everything except you.

4. Everything inside the hula hoop you have 100% control over—this includes you, your thoughts, and your feelings.

5. The next time something bothers you, remember this hula hoop and decide if the problem is something you have control over. If it is (like your feelings), remember that you— and only you—can change it.

SUCCESS SECRET **#14**

It's okay to feel anxious sometimes.

> "It's fine to feel stressed out at times— everyone does. Just remember that learning to relax makes things a lot easier."—*Aidan, age 13*

Emotions can be a big deal. As I've said before, being intense is a normal part of being gifted. That means that feeling overwhelming emotions—both the happy and the sad kind—is normal. The problem isn't that you experience these intense emotions. The problem is in understanding them. Fortunately, one thing you are really good at is figuring things out. The intense stress and anxiety you sometimes feel are normal and not something to freak out over.

SUCCESS SECRET **#15**

You control your feelings, not the other way around.

Learning to manage your emotional intensity begins with learning that your emotions aren't something that just happen without your control. Oh, sure, everyone reacts to things without necessarily being aware of why they are reacting the way they are. That doesn't mean that there isn't a reason for the reaction. There is. You are not a victim of your emotions.

Remember the hula hoop from earlier? Everything outside of the hoop is out of your control, but everything inside is yours to manage. Well, your emotions definitely lie inside the hoop. So, the next time you become overwhelmed by your emotions or scream at your parents for little reason, take a moment to remember that you are in control of your emotions—not the other way around.

> "I hate the out-of-control feeling I get when I have too much to do—tests, projects, friend drama."—*Chandi, age 10*

SUCCESS SECRET #16

Put your feelings into words.

Controlling your emotions begins with recognizing them in the first place. And the best way to recognize them is by developing an emotional vocabulary. This means not only coming up with specific words to label the various feelings you have, but also developing a word or phrase between you, your parents, and perhaps your friends that enables you to communicate when you are overwhelmed. By picking an easy-to-remember word or phrase, you can alert your family and friends that you need help managing your emotions. You can warn them, without getting yourself too stressed, that you aren't able to control all of your emotions at the moment.

For example, let's pretend you have a big project due in school. You are not happy with it and decide to start the whole thing over. The stress from having to redo a project due tomorrow has overwhelmed you. As a result, you yell at your mom when she asks a simple question. Having an emotional vocabulary—words to explain what you're feeling when you can't really explain it—enables you to tell your mom that you need her to not push you. It also enables her to tell you that you seem overwhelmed, just in case the emotions have started to take over without you realizing it.

The development of this vocabulary is a great tool to help you learn how to stay in charge of your emotions. Trust me, your friends and family will appreciate everything you can learn in this area, and so will you. Check out the "Tips for Developing an Emotional Vocabulary."

Tips for Developing an Emotional Vocabulary

1. Pick a word that accurately describes what you're feeling, like "spinning," "bursting," "overwhelmed," or "done."

2. Make the word something simple and easy to remember.

3. Choose the word with your parents. Ask them to help alert you when you are having a hard time managing your emotions.

4. Define what the word means—how the feeling looks. This way everyone has a common language they can use to talk about particular emotions.

5. Define both a word to alert a problem and some general feeling words (e.g., happy, sad, frustrated, anxious). Practice talking about your emotions often.

SUCCESS SECRET **#17**

Learn to calm down before you explode.

Sometimes, despite your best efforts to control your emotions, you can't help it. Your words fail, and you feel yourself edging closer to the point of exploding. It is really important to know how to calm down before you actually explode.

Your brain is a funny thing. When you're too angry (or too sad or too frustrated), the part of your brain that makes rational decisions slows or stops. You literally can't think about calming down (at least not immediately). This is when you must learn to recognize when you're beginning to get angry and calm yourself long enough for your brain to think and relax.

The first step is recognizing how your mind and body tend to react to stress. (We will outline some ways of doing this later in the book.) But, preventing the explosion takes more than just knowing your stress response. It also takes knowing what to do once you are really upset or overwhelmed.

There are lots of tricks people use to calm themselves, like those that were highlighted earlier in the chapter. Things like taking deep breaths, picturing something relaxing, taking a break—all of these things can help diffuse your frustration, anger, or pain and allow your brain time to think before you explode. And, that's the key: giving yourself the time your brain needs to think. Check out the "Tips for Learning to Cool Off" for more ideas.

Tips for Learning to Cool Off

1. Know what makes you upset.
2. Take a deep breath.
3. Count to 10.
4. Walk away from the situation if you can.
5. Find a safe person you can vent to when you are emotionally overwhelmed, like a parent or teacher.

SUCCESS SECRET #18

Learn how to relax.

Perhaps the biggest part of managing your emotions, besides remembering what you can and can't control, is learning to relax. It is only when we are in a relaxed state that we can think clearly enough to discern what's inside the hula hoop from what's outside of our control. Furthermore, it is only when we are relaxed that we can manage our emotions and our behaviors.

Learning to relax requires you to know what it feels like when you are in a calm state, as well as what it feels like when you are not. They more you know about how you feel in these various states, the easier it is to teach yourself to be calm.

The easiest way to discover your own calm state is to define what it means to not be calm. Try watching an action-filled movie. Pay attention to how your body feels. Are you tense? Are your shoulders tight? What about your jaw?

After the movie is over, take stock of your feelings—physical and emotional. Are you tired? Does your body feel looser? Is there still tightness in your shoulders or jaw?

Try this a few times in different situations. After a while, you will be able to recognize both a calm and a not calm state of being.

Once you know what each state feels like, you must learn how to move from one state to the other. Using the Breathing Colors technique (see p. 67), taking a break, and counting to 10 are all ways you can learn to relax. Throughout the book I will list other ways you can learn to calm down.

Once you think you're calm, it is important to make sure. Stress and anxiety can be tricky, sneaking up you when you least expect it. The quiz "Am I Relaxed?" can help you learn how to ensure you are in a calm state.

SUCCESS SECRET #19

You are not your stress.

It is so hard not to define yourself by your feelings. The truth is that you are not your stress. Not at all.

The stress and frustration you feel are just a reaction to a situation you are experiencing. Like you learned with the hula hoop technique, you really have no control over what life throws your way. And although many of the things you experience in the world—the pressure and expectations—may initially stress you out, you do have the ability to change your reactions. To do this, however, you must remember that stress, frustration, and the other things you feel are not the total of who you are.

Remembering this is pretty easy when you're calm. However, remembering it once you are stressed is a lot harder. "The Truth About Me" worksheet is designed to be a reminder about all of the great things you really are, especially during those times when you can't remember!

SUCCESS SECRET #20

Be honest with yourself.

"I hate admitting my mistakes. Or, admitting when I'm stressed. But it's the only way I can learn to control it."—*Alejandro, age 11*

Emotions are often difficult to control because people are so good at lying to themselves about their emotions. Remember how I said that your brain can lie at times? Well, sometimes it lies about our feelings or the feelings of others.

It's really important to be honest with yourself about your feelings. Don't say things are "fine" if they aren't. Likewise, don't create a problem with your

Quiz: Am I Relaxed?

Directions: Circle your answer for each question.

1. Do you have any tension in your body, especially in places like your back, your shoulders, and your jaw?

    yes   no

2. Is your breathing fast?

    yes   no

3. Do you feel hyperfocused and "ready for action"?

    yes   no

4. Are you feeling super happy or super sad?

    yes   no

5. Do you feel like you are ready to explode?

    yes   no

Too many yes answers on this quiz means you are not relaxed. Try a few deep breaths and taking a break. When you're done, ask yourself these questions again.

feelings just to have one. By truthfully looking at how you feel in various situations, you can more easily identify those moments when your emotions are slipping out of control.

Parents and friends can be great allies in helping you become honest about your emotions. Asking them to help you figure out what you're feeling, particularly in times of stress, can go a long way toward learning to identify your emotions for yourself—and more importantly, learning to manage them.

WORKSHEET
The Truth About Me

1. List all of the positive things about you. Be sure to include things from the world of school, the world of friends, and the world of family.

2. Add some nice comments teachers and other adults have said about you.

3. List your goals and dreams for the future.

4. List your favorite things to do with friends and family.

5. After making your lists, take a minute and draw a picture, make a collage, create a playlist, or find another way to illustrate all of the great things you are. Keep the finished product someplace where you can refer to it often, or make several products so you have them at home and at school.

6. Remember to make a new list and a new picture or collage as you change. This way, you will always have a reminder handy of the truth about you as a person.

Parents Sound Off

Parents have a sense of your emotions. They know how hard it can be to manage and control the turbulent wave of feelings that you sometimes experience. Talk to your parents about their thoughts regarding your emotions. Do their comments look like these?

- "(My child) is intensely connected with the world, her friends, and family."—*Kathy*
- "Just my prodding to get (my child) to talk is enough to make her upset and start crying, like she assumes there must be something wrong if I'm prodding her about it."—*Sato*
- "Sometimes it is so hard to know how to help my children with their emotions. They are so hard on themselves, so explosive, so sensitive—some days just saying 'Hi' is enough to set them off."—*Erica*
- "Dealing with my child when she shuts down is so hard. Nothing I say seems to help. I worry about her self-esteem over the long run as I watch her struggle to manage her emotions."—*Lara*
- "The emotional part is the hardest for us to handle. We just get worried when we see our son stress so much over school. We want to make everything easier, but we know that may not be the best thing for him."—*Xan and Kat*

It can be difficult to remember that your parents are your allies in your journey to self-awareness and accepting your emotional intensity. Take a moment to talk with them about your feelings. Together you can learn to not only manage your intensity, but embrace it as well.

Managing your emotions may be one of the hardest things you learn in this journey of discovering the deeper you, but it is also one of the most rewarding. By learning all of the wonderful things your emotions are telling you and facing each feeling with bravery and confidence, you will learn to be the master of your passions—and you will go far!

What Do You Think?

It's time for you to reflect on your feelings and what they mean to you. Take a few moments and think about the following questions.

How do you demonstrate your emotional intensity? Is it something that bothers you at all?

What are the best ways for you to calm down and relax?

What are your tricks for managing your feelings?

INTENSITIES AS STRENGTHS

Chapter 2 talked about your emotional intensity. That isn't the only area of intensity you may show. There are several areas of intensity that may be part of what makes you, you. Things like a strong imagination, super sensitive hearing,

"For a while, I thought that feeling really intense emotions all of the time was a bad thing. That it meant that something was wrong with me. Now I'm learning that my intensities are just part of being gifted—it's part of who I am and what makes me, me."—*Jerome, age 12*

and needing to move for the sake of moving may all be part of your attributes. These areas of intensity may be something you like about yourself. And they may be things you hate. Often you may feel a love-hate relationship with these parts of being you. Regardless, having a variety of areas of intensity is a common part of being gifted. It's important to know both the benefits and strengths of these attributes, as well as some of the drawbacks.

 DOI: 10.4324/9781003232575-5

The next set of success tips is all about understanding all of your unique intensities and fully accepting what it means to be gifted.

SUCCESS SECRET **#21**

Understand the good and not-so-good of your intensities.

As you know, giftedness means a lot more than your scores on tests or your report card. It is about a collection of attributes that capture how your mind works, your emotions, and other areas of overexcitability that you may demonstrate. To best understand your intensities and how they may impact you, it is important to know the characteristics of the different areas of intensity and how each area may look in you.

Check out Table 3: Understanding Intensities. Which of these different intensities describe you? Then, take the quiz "Me and My Intensities" and begin to get familiar with all that giftedness means for you.

SUCCESS SECRET **#22**

Use your gifts kindly.

Sometimes kids are embarrassed about being identified as gifted or worried that it makes them different in a bad way. Others are excited about the label—too excited. Kids will sometimes boast about being the smartest in the class or the only one who knows the rules to all of the games.

The truth is, everyone has something to learn—even gifted kids. More importantly, being gifted is not an excuse for being mean. No one's needs are more or less important than anyone else's. So, use your giftedness kindly—to help others and yourself. Being gifted is special and should not be used to hurt or demean anyone else.

> "Don't brag and feel all smart, because really, you're no different than other gifted kids. And, there are a lot of gifted kids."—*Maya, age 12*

TABLE 3
Understanding Intensities

Dabrowski's Overexciteabilities (Alias et al., 2013)

Domain	Attributes
Psycho-motor	Excessive movement Excessive speech patterns
Sensual	Highly sensitive to environment Sensory dysregulation
Intellectual	Creative problem solvers High degree of concentration on preferred activities Strong memory, especially visual
Imaginational	Strong imagination skills Good at creating fantasy May retreat into imaginary world when bored or upset
Emotional	Complex emotions at a young age Physical reactions to emotional states Intense

Note. Adapted from Fonseca, 2016.

SUCCESS SECRET #23

Embrace your giftedness.

Being identified as gifted is neither a good thing nor a bad thing. It simply is. The label doesn't define you—the characteristics you demonstrate every day do. The key is to embrace all of the aspects of your giftedness and learn how to manage those things that are sometimes hard. These things can include emotional intensity, peer problems, and expectations—yours and those from the people around you. Check out the "Tips for Reaching Your Potential."

Quiz: Me and My Intensities

Directions: Think about your life in general. Read each statement and decide how it applies to you. Circle the appropriate number. Add up the total in each section.

Intellectual Intensity					
	Nothing like me	*Not much like me*	*Neither like me nor not like me*	*Somewhat like me*	*Completely like me*
I love to solve all sorts of puzzles.	1	2	3	4	5
I love to solve mysteries.	1	2	3	4	5
I can concentrate on things I enjoy for very long periods of time.	1	2	3	4	5
Learning is something I enjoy.	1	2	3	4	5
I can often remember things that I see in great detail.	1	2	3	4	5
TOTAL					

Emotional Intensity					
	Nothing like me	*Not much like me*	*Neither like me nor not like me*	*Somewhat like me*	*Completely like me*
My emotions are often deep and intense.	1	2	3	4	5
My emotions can be extreme, ranging from very happy to deeply sad.	1	2	3	4	5
I prefer deep friendships/relationships with people.	1	2	3	4	5
I often get headaches, stomachaches, or heart palpitations in response to stress.	1	2	3	4	5
My emotions are often complex and layered.	1	2	3	4	5
TOTAL					

Quiz: Me and My Intensities, continued

Psychomotor Intensity					
	Nothing like me	*Not much like me*	*Neither like me nor not like me*	*Somewhat like me*	*Completely like me*
I need to move often.	1	2	3	4	5
I learn best when physical movement is involved.	1	2	3	4	5
I often engage in zealous or highly animated speech.	1	2	3	4	5
I struggle to remain still.	1	2	3	4	5
I will often engage in compulsive talking when under stress.	1	2	3	4	5
TOTAL					

Sensual Intensity					
	Nothing like me	*Not much like me*	*Neither like me nor not like me*	*Somewhat like me*	*Completely like me*
I am deeply moved by the arts and nature.	1	2	3	4	5
Loud noises and bright colors can often be bothersome to me.	1	2	3	4	5
I am often impacted by the scent of things.	1	2	3	4	5
I often have strong emotional reactions to music or the arts.	1	2	3	4	5
I will typically seek out or completely withdraw from sensory stimulation when under stress or overwhelmed.	1	2	3	4	5
TOTAL					

Quiz: Me and My Intensities, continued

Imaginational Intensity					
	Nothing like me	*Not much like me*	*Neither like me nor not like me*	*Somewhat like me*	*Completely like me*
I often daydream.	1	2	3	4	5
I have a strong imagination and enjoy imaginational play.	1	2	3	4	5
I often dream.	1	2	3	4	5
I love to read and/or get lost in my own imagination.	1	2	3	4	5
When bored or stressed, I will "disappear" into my imagination.	1	2	3	4	5
TOTAL					

Once you've finished each section, add together the total. Which is your highest or lowest area?

Highest area:_____   Lowest area:_____

SUCCESS SECRET #24

Remember to have fun.

Like it or not, being gifted is nothing you can change. It's something you must learn to embrace. And, it's one of the many things that make you . . . YOU. Learn about what giftedness means for you. Learn to live to your potential. But, remember that you are first and foremost a kid—be sure to have fun every day.

"Remember, you're still a kid. Have fun!"—*Kana, age 10*

Tips for Reaching Your Potential

1. Get to know everything about yourself—the good and the not-so-good.

2. Try something new, such as reading something different or building something you didn't think you could complete.

3. Do something creative every day.

4. Learn something new every day.

5. Instead of saying, "That can't be done," figure out how it can be done.

SUCCESS SECRET **#25**

Believe in yourself.

All in all, being gifted is a really cool thing. However, the traits that make you gifted are the very things that can become a problem for you. The intensity of your thinking can enable you to figure out the really hard stuff—and make school feel boring at times. The strong opinions you hold can make you a leader in class—and cause you to appear bossy and like a know-it-all to your friends. The strong emotions you feel every day can give you a sense of passion and empathy about your world—and turn you into the occasional emotional mess. The trick is learning to balance out the way you're hardwired, using the good aspects of gifted-ness to smooth out the areas in which you struggle.

> "Sometimes it is hard to believe I am smart, especially if I get something wrong on a test. That's when I have to try to remember that everyone gets things wrong sometimes."—*Mia, age 9*

SUCCESS SECRET **#26**

Let go of the little things that annoy you.

Living life as an intense person isn't always easy. You may feel high levels of stress. You may get annoyed with other people—a lot! Learning to embrace your intensities means learning to let go of the little things that annoy you. Have you ever noticed that most of the things you are annoyed about are little? They are things like the way your sibling acts toward you, what a teacher said about your paper, or maybe even something a friend said at lunch.

At the time, these things seem very important. They have the power to put you in a good mood or stress you out enough that your mood is horrible. After a little while, you begin to realize that you are stressing out over something that you have no control over, something you can't really do anything about.

It is at this point you need to learn to let it go and focus on the things you can do, like changing your reaction. Sure, you may always instinctively get hurt when others treat you badly. When you stop to think about it, the only thing you have control over in the situation is your reaction, so keep your focus there. Learn to let go of the other things. You will achieve a lot more balance that way.

> "Don't beat yourself up over the little things—it'll only make you sick." —*Julianne, age 13*

SUCCESS SECRET **#27**

Release your stress.

With all of your intensities, it is not surprising that you may experience periods of stress, anxiety, and overwhelm from time to time. It's essential to learn how to let go of that stress and anxiety when needed. Just as the previous success secrets discussed letting go of the little things, learning to release your sense of overwhelm is also important.

Release doesn't mean ignore. You never want to ignore what you're feeling, which includes big or difficult emotions—things like sadness, grief, and fear. It is important to feel your feelings and not detach. But it is equally important to not get stuck in your emotions. Recognize what you are feeling and learn what to do to regulate your emotional system and tame the intensities that may be out of balance. The following tip sheet may help you when you find yourself struggling to release and regulate.

Tips for Releasing Your Stress

Try these activities to help release the hold of stress or anxiety.

- Take a deep breath.
- Stretch your arms and legs.
- Smile and laugh.
- Take a coloring break.
- Take a walk outside.
- Clean and declutter your room.
- Brush your pet's fur.
- Practice mindful breathing.

SUCCESS SECRET #28

Embrace your intensity.

Being intense in thinking, in your physical reactions to things, and in your emotions is not a bad thing. In fact, it is the very thing that can make you excel. If you think of it differ-

> "Like it or not, I know that I am a pretty intense person. I might as well figure out how to deal with it."—*Peter, age 12*

ently, *intensity* is just another word for *passion*. Passion is what drives the artist to create, the doctor to find a cure, the teacher to teach, and you to learn. Passion is a very good thing. So, embrace your passion and your intensity—it is one of the very best parts of you.

Try completing the worksheet "The Best Me."

Parents Sound Off

Parents have a lot to say about the good and bad aspects of giftedness. Many of them know all too well how hard their children have to work at devel-

WORKSHEET
The Best Me

Directions: Using the intensity quiz you completed earlier, list your areas of intensity from highest to lowest. Identify your strengths and how the areas of intensity could be areas of strength. What do you notice about your strengths?

Intensity Area	Potential Strengths	Thoughts

oping friendships, dealing with emotions, and fighting boredom in school. Take a look at what these parents say about giftedness, and then talk with your parents and see how they feel.

- "I love that my kid thinks of herself as smart. But, she never gives herself any room for failure. Everything has to be perfect. My daughter places unrealistic expectations on herself."—*Lynn*
- "It was so hard watching our children not live up to their potential because they were bored and took their education for granted. I think a lot of gifted kids do that."—*Rajas*
- "I love that no matter what she does, I know she'll give it her all. (But) I worry that she doesn't give herself permission to fail."—*Carol*
- "Man, parenting our children is great—and miserable at the same time. It is so hard to know how to help our children control their emotions or give themselves a break periodically."—*Andie*
- "I wish my daughter saw her strengths they way I do. She seems to only focus on the more negative aspects of herself—of being gifted."—*LaShon*

Overall, parents see the ways you struggle to manage your intensities. They also see all of the great tasks you can accomplish with your incredible mind.

In the end, all of the attributes of giftedness—the way you think, feel, and behave—are the things that make you amazing. Those same attributes are also the things that make life hard at times. Your job is to figure out how to keep it all in balance.

What Do You Think?

It's time for you to take a moment and reflect on the ideas in this chapter and your own thoughts. Figure out what your best attributes are and which ones cause you the most grief. This is the first step toward understanding how to maintain a good balance.

What are the ways in which you demonstrate your giftedness?
How do you think, act, and feel about things?

What aspects of your giftedness give you the most trouble?

How can you stay in balance?

GIFTED AT SCHOOL

You spend more than half of your life either at school or doing school-related things. Homework, tests, projects—it's all part of the school experience. For gifted kids, this is both a good thing and a bad thing.

Hardwired to learn easily, some of you excel at school—pushing yourselves to achieve consistently. Others of you do only what you need to get by. Still others of you struggle. Whether you are a high-achieving gifted kid or one who struggles, you are all likely to experience both highs and lows when it comes to school. The next few chapters will cover the most typical problems that arise in your school experience: motivation, the pressure to perform, and social mishaps.

Let's start off with a little quiz to test your knowledge about academics and giftedness. Hang on to your answers for now, but be sure to come back after reading this section to see if any of your answers have changed.

DOI: 10.4324/9781003232575-6

Quiz: Giftedness and School

Directions: Circle your answer for each question.

1. Being gifted means homework should not take very long.

    true   *false*

2. Mistakes mean I am not as smart as I thought I was.

    true   *false*

3. Because I'm gifted, I don't need to study as much as most people.

    true   *false*

4. There is nothing I can do about the pressure I feel at school.

    true   *false*

5. Because I'm gifted, my teachers should expect that I will do well.

    true   *false*

Chapter 4

BORING ASSIGNMENTS AND HUM-DRUM DAYS

Most people assume that gifted kids have it easy in school. You know this isn't always true, understanding that the routine nature of school can make it boring to you. Repetitive assignments often feel like torture, and minutes of simple work can easily turn into hours.

> "I can't lie—I really don't like school. I love learning new things, and I love learning how things work. But school? It always feels so repetitive and boring to me."—*Anthony, age 10*

One of the biggest issues all school-aged children face is homework—the task that many parents and children dread. Instead of simply being practice for the concepts taught in school, homework has turned into a battle zone for many households—maybe even yours.

The problem with homework and gifted kids usually boils down to this: Homework is repetitive, rote work that you may have already mastered, or

 DOI: 10.4324/9781003232575-7

it is vague and filled with open-ended questions that you aren't certain you understand clearly. The result in both situations is the same: Work that was designed to be a quick and simple review of concepts taught in school turns into an ordeal that is typically filled with strong emotional reactions. You and your parents are often left feeling frustrated, angry, and exhausted.

Perhaps the school concerns you have aren't limited to homework time. Perhaps school, itself, leaves you wondering, "Is this all there is to life?" The tips throughout this chapter address the often frustrating experience of school and things you can do to make it all better.

SUCCESS SECRET #29

Not all teachers understand giftedness.

Guess what? Not all teachers understand giftedness. In fact, most teachers don't really know what it means to be gifted. Like many people, sometimes they think it means you will be a high achiever. If you're not, they may think you aren't really gifted. As you already know, this just isn't true. Giftedness is all about potential and attributes. If you find that your teacher struggles with understanding your particular brand of giftedness, hang in there and just keep doing your best. Try talking to the teacher or your parents. Sometimes you have to explain yourself to others in order to get your needs met. Check out the "Tips for Talking to Teachers."

SUCCESS SECRET #30

Start with the easy stuff.

"I like to get the easy stuff out of the way first, before I work on stuff that takes longer."—*Maka, age 9*

Have you ever sat down to do your homework, only to find you were confused on the very first thing you attempted? Moments like these are enough to turn homework time into a nightmare. Instead of getting frustrated and spending hours on the things that confuse you, why not skip ahead to something easy? In fact, go through your

Tips for Talking to Teachers

1. Ask them when you can speak to them about school.

2. State your concerns clearly.

3. Avoid words that blame, such as "You did this," or "You never do that."

4. Use "I" statements, such as, "I would like to know if I can have a different word list," or "Sometimes I do better with more challenging work."

5. Ask your parents to help you if you are afraid to approach your teacher.

work and get all of the easy, fast stuff out of the way. Make a list of questions on the harder things that confuse you. Once you relax, you will likely find that you understand a lot more than you realize. Try it out the next time you find yourself frustrated with your homework. My guess is that you'll get through the work a lot faster.

SUCCESS SECRET #31

Always give 100%.

Sometimes gifted kids assume that because they are smart and most things come very easily to them, homework will be a breeze. You may feel this way as well. The truth is, being smart isn't enough to have success in school. It also takes discipline, self-control, and commitment.

This is especially true when it comes to work that feel repetitive or boring. When things come easily to you, it is natural to want to kick back and let things

> "Just because you are gifted, doesn't mean you shouldn't work hard."
> —Leif, age 13

slide. Over time, you may stop giving schoolwork your all and settle for less than you are capable of achieving. Eventually, giving less than 100% becomes a habit. Giving less than 80% can become a habit as well. And, sooner or later, you may stop caring altogether.

What happens when things get harder, which they always do at some point? What then? If you're already in the habit of giving less than your best, then you will struggle when things get harder. Confronted with difficult work without the necessary work habits to persevere can leave you feeling like a failure—and all because you became comfortable with giving less than your best.

I don't know about you, but that seems like a very bad plan to me.

The easiest way to fix the problem is to never settle for less than your very best. Give 100% in everything you do and try. That way when things get hard, you will have the necessary drive and perseverance to push through the difficult work until it becomes easy.

SUCCESS SECRET **#32**

Don't overthink things.

It is very easy for gifted kids to overthink things. This usually happens because your brain is working so hard and fast all of the time. As a result, you often think things are more complex than they are, believing that nothing can be as easy as it seems to you. You are always looking for the trick.

> "My brain is always thinking about a million different things."—*Maddy, age 13*

Guess what? There rarely is a trick. Sometimes the easy answer really *is* the answer.

Let me give you an example of how you may be overthinking things. Let's say the teacher gives an assignment to write a short paragraph stating the color of the sky. Most students will go home and write a few sentences that basically say the color of the sky is blue.

Not you—you will struggle with the assignment, wondering what time of day you're supposed to look at the sky, whether or not there are any clouds, or what the moisture content of the atmosphere is at that time. Because you did not get clarification on the assignment, you will think and think and think—trying to riddle out what the teacher is actually looking for.

This may take hours and many, many tears.

In the end, you will likely write several pages explaining how you can't possibly answer the question without knowing more information. What do you think the teacher actually wanted? That's right—a few sentences saying the sky is blue.

Overthinking without getting clarification will almost always lead to more frustration. Think about that the next time you begin to spin and decide if it's really worth it.

SUCCESS SECRET **#33**

Accepting help is a smart thing to do.

Overthinking is really only a problem when you don't seek clarification—when you don't ask for help. But, sometimes, help is offered even when you don't ask. And sometimes, you really do need the help. Yet, as with most gifted kids, you are reluctant to accept help, thinking it makes you look less gifted somehow. Or, maybe you think that accepting help makes you less perfect—an idea that may cause literal pain.

The truth is that everyone needs help from time to time. Accepting it when it is offered is the key to making the most of your giftedness. No one really expects you to know everything all of the time. So, when your teachers offer clarification or your parents offer help, hear them out. You may learn an unexpected tip that makes everything a lot easier for you. Even if you don't learn anything this time, you are opening yourself up to future learning—and that is always a smart thing to do.

> "Teachers are there to help you. Don't shut them out. It won't help."—*Jin, age 11*

SUCCESS SECRET **#34**

Balance out the hard with the easy.

Remember when I said it was important to start with easy problems first? There is a reason for this—it is important for gifted kids to feel some success with working on tasks. This applies to both tests and the other work you do. If you only tackle the hard stuff, you will likely get frustrated to the point of giving up.

Balancing out the things that are hard for you to finish with the things that are easier is a great way to prevent this frustration overload. Start with something easy. Then do something harder. Alternate between easy and hard until everything is finished.

The other possibility is to complete everything that is easy first, as stated earlier in this chapter. This works particularly well on a test. But, with most work, alternating between easy and hard is actually better. It allows you to spread out the things that are going to give you the most difficulty.

Some days everything feels hard. This usually happens when you are struggling with your motivation. Maybe you are tired, or maybe you are overwhelmed. Either way, finding the desire to complete your work is hard.

On those days, it is essential to start with the easy things and build momentum. As you complete your tasks, crossing them off your to-do list, you will find your motivation returning. Before you know it, you will finish everything you had to do—without the tears and frustration that have occurred in the past.

> "Being motivated to do the hard stuff can be so difficult at times. So can staying motivated to do the easy stuff. I guess motivation is just a hard thing."—*Maria, age 11*

SUCCESS SECRET **#35**

Learn how to ask for what you need.

Yes, there are times when school and your assignments may feel too easy and not relevant. This doesn't mean you have to just deal with it. You can learn how to ask teachers for what you need—whether that means harder or more interesting assignments or something easier if you are struggling. The first step is learning when and how to ask for what you need.

Known as self-advocacy, asking for what you need is an important skill to learn for school and for later in life. This same skill can help you land an exciting job or opportunity, get your needs met in relationships, and manage your health and well-being. Self-advocacy requires being able to determine what you need and who can help you. It also requires taking a risk and recovering when the answer is "no." Finally, self-advocacy demands perseverance and a willingness to stick with an idea even when it is hard. Check out the "Tips for Asking the Teacher for What You Want."

Tips for Asking the Teacher for What You Want

Keep the following ideas in mind when asking your teacher for things:

- Know your strengths and areas of opportunity when you talk with your teacher.
- Identify your needs and why the current work doesn't meet your needs.
- Be polite and calm when asking for things.
- Be willing to work harder or do more.
- Explain your point of view clearly.
- Accept "no" if your teacher denies your request.
- Keep asking for what you need.

Note that self-advocacy is not an excuse to be rude to your teachers or parents. Nor is it a reason to not do what others have asked of you. Teachers will be more willing to adjust your assignments if you are polite when asking. They are also going to be more open to your ideas if you demonstrate that you understand their assigned work. Remember, being respectful can go a long way when working with teachers and parents alike.

SUCCESS SECRET #36

Every experience has something to offer.

As I mentioned in the previous success secret, sometimes you may hear the word "no." You may get stuck doing an assignment that is very easy or working on something that seems unimportant to you. This is when you need to remember that every experience you have can be of benefit to you. I know that seems wrong. After all, how is doing repetitive work beneficial to you? How is learning about something you already know helpful? If you open up your mind, you may discover that doing that repetitive work enabled you to improve the speed of your skills. Or maybe learning something you already knew taught you a little bit about patience.

Try to go into every experience believing that there is something you can learn. Often just adapting your mindset to this type of thinking is enough to open your thinking to new possibilities. You never know where sudden insights and new knowledge will come. Being open-minded and optimistic is a great way to set the stage for enjoying more of what life has to offer. Read the "Tips for Developing Optimism."

Parents Sound Off

Parents are as frustrated as you are when it comes to homework. They express concern about the time it takes to complete homework, the emotional drama that often happens when students get overwhelmed, and the stress they feel from you. At the same time, parents understand the role homework plays in helping you build responsibility. The quotes below express some of their concerns and feelings about homework time.

- "Homework that is repetitive and goes nowhere, and the notion that she needs to do everything perfectly and on time, is difficult and frustrating for her."—*Yeida*
- "Homework time can be a nightmare in our house. Other times it is no problem at all. It just depends on what the kids have going on, how tired we all are, and whether or not they understand the work."—*Jonathan*
- "Homework is 'busy work,' and she doesn't enjoy doing it, but we can make it more challenging for her by just asking her more difficult questions"—*Thomas*
- "Homework is a challenge for my daughter, who insists on going above and beyond in her work and producing perfect handwriting every time. This can make homework take a long time to finish."—*Tiare*
- "I just don't know about homework and school these days. It all seems too easy for my son and causes so much drama in our house."—*Geoff*

Ask your parents if these quotes reflect some of the ways they feel. What can you do together to make homework less of a nightmare in your home? While you're at it, talk with your parents about school in general. Let them know the things you like, as well as the things that are frustrating to you. It could spark a few very important conversations.

Tips for Developing Optimism

The following ideas can help you develop a more optimistic perspective:

- Find something positive about the day—every day.
- Keep track of the things you are grateful for.
- Point out the strengths in others—and in yourself.
- When you struggle, remember that it will pass. Things do get better.
- Whenever you think you can't, add the word "yet" . . . "I can't, yet."

What Do You Think?

Take a few minutes to think about your feelings regarding school and homework, and then answer the following questions.

How long does it take you to finish your classwork and homework (on average)? Do you think this is a long time or a short time, compared to your friends?

What is the hardest part of homework time . . . the workload . . . the boredom factor . . . the planning aspect?

How can you solve the problems listed above? Discuss these solutions with your parents and turn homework time into something productive and not something that is filled with arguments or tears. Try some of the same strategies with your schoolwork, as needed.

5

MOTIVATION, PERFECTIONISM, AND OTHER DILEMMAS

I have a question for you—do you tend to measure how smart you are in terms of how easy everything is? I bet you do. In fact, you probably also believe that long, complicated assignments that you have a hard time with are either bad assignments

> "I am really hard on myself. I expect that I am supposed to be perfect in everything. So if I'm not, I can't really handle it. I know that I shouldn't feel that way, but yeah, I am struggling with that. Still."—*Rebecca, age 13*

(the teacher messed up) or proof that you are not really as smart as everyone thinks you are.

Actually, neither assumption is true. Your intellectual abilities and your school performance seldom relate directly to one another. Yes, it's true that most assignments will come more easily to you because you are smart. But, if your teacher is doing a good job in challenging you, you should find yourself

 DOI: 10.4324/9781003232575-8

having to really work on some things in class. Believing that working hard in school means you aren't smart is a false assumption and something you will need to change if you are going to reach your potential.

Assignments can seem hard for a few reasons, many of them related to the attributes of giftedness we've already discussed. For example, sometimes an assignment seems a lot harder than the teacher meant it to be. Why? Because you read too much into the assignment. You are overthinking it. You believed the teacher was asking you for something far more complicated than was intended. This can lead to endless hours of work and a lot of emotional angst.

The following tips all focus on motivation, perfectionism, and the other things that can make school feel more frustrating then it needs to be.

SUCCESS SECRET #37

Don't put off your projects.

Projects, weekly assignments, and long-term tests are the things most gifted kids tend to overlook when planning out their homework. I can understand why: If it isn't due right away, then you tend to forget about it. Plus, it's easy to forget to write it down as part of your homework.

Here's the problem with that: Although you may work quickly and need to study less than someone who is not gifted, you will easily become overwhelmed if you leave things until the last minute.

The solution? Plan out all of the tasks that aren't due the following day. This includes projects, weekly homework packets, tests, and anything else that you have multiple days to complete.

> "Waiting to the last minute to do your work only makes you more stressed. Try to get things done early. You'll sleep better." —*Chandler, age 13*

The easiest way to get this done is to break the task down into small parts. If it's a weekly homework packet, decide which pages you will complete each night to make sure the packet is done on time. If it's a test, then decide which things you will study each night and how you'll study. (Will you review your notes . . . use flashcards?) If it's a project, then break down the task into smaller ones—research, writing, assembling the project itself—and decide which part you are doing each night.

Many of you will have teachers or parents who break this stuff down for you. Although it's wonderful that they are willing to do that, the responsibility is ultimately yours. You are the one in school. You are the one earning the grades. Eventually, when you move into higher grades, your teachers and parents won't break your assignments down for you. So, the sooner you learn how to do it, the better. And when you're an adult, you will need this same type of strategy for your job.

After you have broken down the various tasks, write what you are going to achieve each day in your planner or on a calendar. When it is time to draft a nightly homework plan, be sure to include these items on your list.

Breaking down tasks and making lists is a great way to keep your homework under control and maintain your emotional balance—no matter how busy you may feel.

SUCCESS SECRET **#38**

Know who you can call if you get stuck.

Sometimes things go wrong despite your best efforts to write things down and make a plan. Maybe you lose your planner, you're not at school, or you just forgot to make sure you were prepared. Hey, it happens to everyone sooner or later. The important thing to remember is to stay calm and have a Plan B—an emergency plan.

Emergency plans are just that—your plan for what to do when things go wrong. You still have to complete your work, even when things go bad. So how are you going to do that when you don't have any idea of what to do?

This is when you need to call a friend, look up the homework on the school's website, or figure out another way to get the job done. Part of being a successful student means knowing how to navigate through an emergency when it happens.

Make a list of all of the ways you can get answers to homework and other school questions. Think about the ways your school offers help for students who have forgotten their homework, as well as which friends may have the information you need. Keep a few copies of this list in important places, including your backpack, your homework study space, with your parents, and near the phone.

Emergencies will happen. Being prepared can keep the emergency from turning into a disaster. Try completing the worksheet "My Homework Emergency List."

SUCCESS SECRET **#39**

Perfection is a myth.

Perfectionism has a bad rap in our culture. We often define perfectionism as the need to be or appear perfect in everything you do, never making a mistake on anything. And, it's totally unrealistic. No one is perfect, and striving for constant perfection is the quickest way to getting yourself overwhelmed, especially on your schoolwork.

Feeling the need for perfection, however, is very common with gifted kids, even though it is unrealistic. That is because of the high performance standards that comes with being gifted. This need to do really well on everything often comes out as perfectionism. It's important to learn to differentiate between trying to do your very best and trying to be perfect. These are two very different things. In the constant pursuit of perfection, kids like you may become afraid to take risks in school, decide not to turn in their work to the teacher for fear that it isn't good enough, or simply become too overwhelmed to even attend school.

So, why do you fall into the perfectionism trap? Most of the time it has to do with your belief that everyone else thinks you have to be perfect if you are gifted. You worry that mistakes will disappoint your teachers, your parents, even your friends. And as a result, you allow yourself to believe that the only way to make sure you don't disappoint anyone is to be perfect.

Man, that's an impossible task to give yourself. No wonder you and other gifted kids feel so much stress most of the time.

A better way to deal with the pressures of being gifted is to remember that learning is a process. Your parents know this, as do your teachers. They really don't expect you to know everything instantly. They understand that learning takes time and that it is through your mistakes that a deeper understanding of things occurs.

Teachers and parents will often sit with kids when a mistake is made and re-explain the lessons being taught. The problem is, you may look at this as if they are disappointed. Nothing is further from the truth. They're just trying to guide you to knowledge—teach you how to look at your mistakes

WORKSHEET
My Homework Emergency List

1. What methods does your school offer for finding out about homework in an emergency? I've listed a couple that may apply. Cross out the ones your school does not offer, and list others I may have left off.

    a. Class website

    b. School website

    c. _____

    d. _____

    e. _____

2. List at least three friends who may know the homework for the night. If you have multiple teachers, try to list at least three friends for each teacher and class.

Friend	Class	Phone Number/ Email Address

3. Ask your friends for a phone number so you can text or call in an emergency. Be sure to make sure your parents are okay with you getting or giving out your phone number before you complete this step.

4. Brainstorm other possible homework emergency solutions with your parents. Write down your most feasible ideas.

5. Remember to keep copies of your list in several places, including:
    a. in your backpack,
    b. in your homework study space, and
    c. on your computer or smartphone's notes app.

as opportunities to grow. Trust me, they aren't expecting you to be perfect and know everything. Try practicing the "Tips for Beating the Perfectionism Trap."

SUCCESS SECRET **#40**

Mistakes are opportunities to learn.

Speaking of mistakes, did you know that mistakes are actually just opportunities to learn? Many of the things we use every day were discovered or invented as a direct result of a mistake. It's true. By taking risks and trying new things, you will often make mistakes. Sometimes those mistakes can lead to amazing discoveries and enable you to think of new things that you never considered before. But, if you aren't willing to take a risk, if you get too stuck on your perfectionism to be willing to make a mistake, you may be missing out on an amazing opportunity to learn something new.

Look at Table 4: "Amazing Discoveries That Came From Mistakes"—everything on it was discovered by accident, either when a scientist was looking for something else or when someone was just messing around. Amazing, right? Where would we be without the accidental discovery of the Americas, the medicine we use for diabetes, or even sticky notes?

Quite an amazing list, isn't it? Without taking risks and being willing to fail, most of these things would have never been discovered or created. What additional things could you add to the list?

Be willing to take risks, and who knows—maybe your mistakes will lead to a great invention too.

SUCCESS SECRET **#41**

Take the time to think through a difficult problem.

Do you have a hard time working through difficult problems? I know a lot of gifted children who do. Maybe it's because it is scary to face a hard problem and the idea that you could fail. Maybe it has to do with the horrible feeling you can get in the pit of your stomach when you're confronted with something you don't instinctively know how to do. And, maybe it's because you'll

Tips for Beating the Perfectionism Trap

1. Make of list of the things you think need to be perfect (e.g., homework, answers on tests).

2. Set goals for yourself regarding homework and other things. Ask yourself if the goals are realistic to achieve. Show them to your parents or teachers to make sure they are reasonable.

3. Focus on the process of learning, not the grades.

4. Practice the PROOF technique. Use it as a way to help you make sure you are looking at the situation realistically.

5. Ask yourself these questions whenever you are getting stressed about making mistakes:
   a. Is what I am feeling realistic? (Use the PROOF technique to find out.)
   b. Are my goals reasonable?
   c. What would happen if I failed?
   d. Can I change how I am feeling? (Remember the hula hoop technique.)

Go through these tips frequently until you've made a habit of working past your perfectionism tendencies.

---

avoid that stuck feeling at all costs, even if it means blowing off something you need to finish.

Regardless of your reasons, solving difficult problems can be one of the most challenge things about the world of school. Take a look at the "Tips for Solving Problems" and try them the next time you get stuck.

SUCCESS SECRET #42

When in doubt, ask.

Ah yes, asking questions—the most difficult thing in the world for many gifted kids. Most of you will avoid it completely, deciding to figure out something on your own rather than asking a question and appearing like you don't have all of the answers after all.

TABLE 4
Amazing Discoveries That Came From Mistakes

1. An inventor was experimenting with a new type of vacuum tube. It eventually became the first microwave (Prabhune, 2015).
2. Medicines, including penicillin, the smallpox vaccine, and Coumadin, all widely used now, were discovered by scientists who were looking for other things (Banner, 2008).
3. A cook in China discovered fireworks when he accidentally mixed three common kitchen items (HowStuffWorks, 2007).
4. Play-Doh was created by accident when Noah and Joseph McVicker were trying to make wallpaper cleaner. It was later sold to a toy company (HowStuffWorks, 2007).
5. Post-It Notes were conceived by Arthur Fry as a way to keep bookmarks in hymnals and combined with an accidental invention of an adhesive made by 3M employee Spencer Silver (HowStuffWorks, 2007).

The reality is, taking 3 times longer to do something because you were afraid to seek clarification is sillier than appearing like you need help—a lot sillier. You've probably heard the statement "There are no stupid questions except the ones not asked"—this is exactly what we are talking about here. You must be willing to risk appearing foolish if you are going to learn. And this means you must ask questions.

Why? If for no other reason than to make sure you understand what you are being asked to do. Oftentimes gifted kids stress out over assignments simply because they got home without knowing what the teacher wanted from them. Had they asked, there would have been no confusion, and homework time would have gone more smoothly.

So, do yourself a favor the next time you are uncertain about something—an assignment in school or a chore at home—and ask questions. Keep asking until you understand what you are supposed to be doing. If you don't ask, everyone will assume you understand things and will expect you to be able to do the work assigned.

"Be willing to talk to your teachers and ask for help on things, even if the other kids in the class laugh."—*Erika, age 11*

Tips for Solving Problems

1. First you must relax. Practice the relaxation strategies from Chapter 2.

2. Read through the question carefully. Make notes, if needed, about what the question is asking.

3. Brainstorm solutions. Evaluate your solutions to see if they work and make logical sense.

4. Pick a solution and apply it to the problem. If it doesn't work, repeat the process with a different solution.

5. When in doubt, ask for help.

SUCCESS SECRET #43

You cannot think when you are frustrated.

Earlier, we talked about stress and how it impacts your ability to think. Guess what? The same applies to frustration. This is because feeling frustrated is another part of a stress response.

Frustration typically results when you feel disappointment in something or someone. It can happen when you try to do something and can't, like when you have a difficult problem on a test and can't figure it out, or

> "Freaking out before a test can make you do worse. I used to cry before tests, and it felt like I couldn't think right. It took a while, but I learned to get past it." —*Tatianna, age 13*

when you try to explain something to someone and they don't understand you, no matter how hard you are trying. The feelings that arise in these situations can usually be defined as frustration.

Just like with stress, when you are frustrated you are not going to think clearly. Usually, you are going to get stuck in the frustration and have a hard time moving your thoughts to anything other than the feelings you have about the frustration, feelings that can include sadness, anger, and deep disappointment.

It is important to remember to relax as soon as you feel the frustration starting. Remind yourself that the feelings will pass if you remember to relax.

SUCCESS SECRET **#44**

Always remember to breathe.

Did you know that many people hold their breath when they get emotionally overwhelmed? Did you know that holding your breath keeps your brain from being able to think properly at times? It's not surprising, then, that you may be making really bad decisions when you are overwhelmed.

Deep breathing can help. A lot.

The key to deep breathing, however, is taking enough slow, deep breaths to really calm everything down and reengage the decision-making parts of your brain. This can be challenging for some people. It's hard to know when you have taken enough breaths to reach a calm state, especially if you are really overwhelmed when you start.

That's where the Breathing Colors technique can really help. This strategy is a visual way to see your stress in your imagination and watch it float away. Try the "Tips for Breathing Colors Technique" every time you need to relax. I think you'll be surprised at how effective it can be.

SUCCESS SECRET **#45**

Live to your values.

It can be hard to jump into mundane schoolwork, chores, and other tasks if you are not motivated. This is where your values can help. Values are the attributes you deem as necessary in your life. They could include things like being kind, or being a helper, or being an upstander. When you identify your core values and align those values to the tasks you have to do in life, you can often boost your motivation to complete the various things you may need to do.

Take a look at the list of values on the worksheet "My Obligations and My Values." Circle those values that apply to you. Once you've figured out some of your values, list your different tasks based on your level of motivation to

Tips for the Breathing Colors Technique

1. Take several deep breaths.

2. On the inhalation, picture your favorite color. I use blue or pink.

3. On the exhalation, imagine a muddy-looking color. This is the color of the stress in your body.

4. Continue slow, steady breathing until the color you inhale matches the color you exhale.

5. Make a mental note of how long it took—this will help you learn more about your own feelings and how you respond to things.

---

complete. Take those tasks with the lowest motivation and see if you can align any of your values to the tasks. When you need to complete the various activities, focus on your values and allow that renewed focus to help give you the motivation boost you may need to get through the task. Try this whenever you get stuck.

Parents Sound Off

Parents have a hard time dealing with your perfectionism, too, as well as the stress you show related to that perfectionism. Expectations and pressure are also something parents have a lot of strong feelings about. Read their quotes to get a better sense of what your parents may be thinking about your motivation, perfectionism, and the pressures you deal with every day.

- "My kids think their teachers expect that everything they do will be perfect. Maybe the teachers do feel that way."—*Janice*
- "My kids impose more pressure on themselves than I ever could. In some ways that makes it easy on me. But I hate seeing what it does to them."—*Nellie*
- "My kids are both different in how the pressure they feel looks—my daughter tends to explode, whereas my son implodes. It makes me feel like I am walking on eggshells most of the time, just trying to not make them emotionally crack."—*Kamari*

WORKSHEET
My Obligations and My Values

Part 1

Directions: Read each "value" word. Circle those that best represent the values and feelings you want in your life.

Acceptance	Accomplishment	Acknowledgment	Affection	Alive
Amazing	Appreciation	Awe	Balance	Boldness
Brave	Calm	Capable	Cheerful	Comfortable
Content	Courageous	Creative	Decisive	Determined
Eager	Elated	Elevated	Empowered	Encouraged
Excited	Fabulous	Freedom	Friendship	Fulfillment
Generous	Grace	Grateful	Grounded	Happy
Hopeful	Important	Innovative	Invigorate	Joyful
Kindness	Love	Magical	Nurtured	Optimistic
Powerful	Refreshed	Satisfied	Strong	Treasured
Understood	Vulnerable	Whole		

Part 2

Directions: List the everyday activities and obligations you do regularly. For each activity, choose one or two of the above feelings. Pick those things you want to feel to motivate you to complete the activity.

Activity	Value
Going to lunch with friends	*Friendship, appreciation, love*

Note. Adapted from Fonseca, 2017.

- "(My child) gets frustrated—she is a perfectionist and gets mad if things aren't completely perfect and on time."—*James*
- "Oh yeah, my daughter is definitely a perfectionist. Not just in her schoolwork but in all aspects of her life—school, her room, sports. It can be exhausting."—*Gloria*

Perfectionism, pressure, stress, and frustration—these are all realities in your life. Learning to manage these emotions will not only help you reach your potential, but also give you the tools you will use as an adult to tackle similar feelings.

What Do You Think?

Now it's your turn to think about the your motivation, perfectionism, and the pressures you may feel every day. As with the other chapters, be sure to come back and reflect on these questions throughout the year. What you feel today may be different from your feelings tomorrow.

Do you struggle with trying to be perfect? What strategies can you try to minimize your perfectionism?

Would you say you are highly motivated to do your best? Or, do you struggle with your motivation at times? How can you balance this out in a way that helps you perform your best at school without the overwhelm?

How often do you take breaks, and what do you do during breaks? Do your breaks help to reduce your feelings of frustration regarding school?

Chapter 6

NAVIGATING THE SOCIAL WORLD OF SCHOOL

> "I am really bad at listening to some of my friends. I always feel like I am right—so it's hard to give other kids a chance to speak."—*Nina, age 11*

Friendships are some of the hardest things for gifted kids to learn to navigate. This is particularly true in school settings, where you often have to learn to work in collaborative groups and share responsibilities.

Why are these kinds of settings challenging to manage in the first place? Most gifted kids are natural leaders who believe that their way is the only way to accomplish the task at hand. Like many things with giftedness, the truth isn't so easy. Although you may often know the rules to games better than your peers or know how to spot solutions to problems more efficiently than your classmates and friends, that doesn't mean that you are the only one who can figure something out. The trick is learning how to share leadership roles,

DOI: 10.4324/9781003232575-9

bend a little on your ideas, and be willing to let your friends have their say in the activity.

SUCCESS SECRET #46

Not all kids understand giftedness.

Just as teachers sometimes struggle with giftedness, so do kids. This especially may mean your friends who are not identified as gifted. They may have a hard time understanding why you get stressed about your grades or why you seem so sensitive all of the time. They may even get jealous over your strong thinking skills. As a result, some friends may tease you.

> "Just be yourself. If people get stressed over that, that is their deal. You worry about being true to who you are."—*Jared, age 12*

Try not to get upset. Their reaction is no different than your confusion over why they don't worry more about grades or the big issues facing the world. You just view the world through a different lens, focusing on different kinds of things, than they do. This is why it will feel like some of your friends don't "get" you.

Bottom line: Don't try to force your friends to understand your point of view. The trick is learning how to get along despite these differences and understanding that multiple points of view are important.

SUCCESS SECRET #47

Listen to other people's suggestions.

As a kid, even a gifted kid, you have a lot of people offering advice: your teachers, your parents, your siblings, and maybe even your friends. It can be really hard to listen to all of these people. You have your own way of doing things. You know what the assignment is and how you think it should be done.

> "Always listen to your teachers, no matter how boring they may seem. Their words will help you later on."—*Katelyn, age 13*

But, you don't know everything. Sometimes the advice from your parents can help you be better organized. Sometimes the advice from your siblings can keep you out of trouble. And sometimes the advice from teachers can save you hours of work.

Listening to other people's suggestions does not diminish you—it doesn't mean that you don't know things, nor does it mean that you're wrong. All it shows is a willingness on your part to see a different point a view—a willingness to learn.

Trust me, to your teachers, parents, and siblings, being willing to hear something new is definitely a sign of being smart.

SUCCESS SECRET **#48**

Go easy on your friends.

As a gifted kid, you probably can be very hard on yourself, demanding perfection in everything you attempt. This isn't limited to how you treat yourself. You can be equally demanding of your friends, expecting them to hold themselves to the same level of perfection. Although some of your gifted friends may do this, most of your other friends do not. In fact, most people in the world do not hold themselves to that rigid of a standard. They make mistakes, assume things that aren't true, and don't always remember to think of others.

> "Your friends may not always 'get' you—that's okay. Give them a break, they are trying their best."—*Marlene, age 12*

In short, they are human. And, so are you.

Jumping all over your friends when they make mistakes or accidentally hurt you often makes the situation worse. No one likes to have all of their flaws pointed out. I know you don't. So, don't do that to your friends. Go easy on them, and remember—not everyone can do the things you can. It isn't fair to expect that from them.

SUCCESS SECRET **#49**

You don't always have to be right.

Shocking, I know. Just like no one expects you to get straight A's on everything, no one really expects you to be right all of the time. In fact, being wrong occasionally, or even just letting someone else be right, is another thing that makes you smart. It means you are willing to take chances. It also means that you are willing to allow someone else to answer questions in class and be the center of attention.

More than anything, it shows the world that you don't need to be right in order to have value. By allowing others to experience the joy of getting a correct answer or giving yourself permission to not correct someone when you know they are wrong, you are saying that you don't need the approval of others to feel okay. You're saying that it is enough to just be . . . you.

And, you know what? It is!

So, humble yourself from time to time and remember that there will always be someone smarter, faster, and better than you. However, it doesn't matter—because those things do not define who you are on the inside.

> "Don't be a know-it-all with your friends. They are probably just as smart as you are."—*Roberto, age 13*

SUCCESS SECRET **#50**

Respect everyone's ideas.

You like being listened to, don't you? You like having your teacher or parents tell you that you've done something good, right? So do your friends.

It is important as you learn to cultivate friendships that you remember that everyone has a need to feel heard and respected. It's part of being a human being. So, how can you show your friends that you respect them?

Allowing them to say what they think is a good start. Others things, like allowing them to be right, letting them pick a game or activity now and then, and treating them with kindness, are all ways you can show respect to your friends.

By doing this, you are saying to a friend, "I appreciate who you are as a person." It also conveys the message that the person has an important place in your life and that you value them. Mutual respect is the key to any true friendship. Without it, there is no trust. And without trust, the foundation for the friendship will crumble.

Take the quiz "Are These Signs of Respect?" to test your respect know-how.

SUCCESS SECRET #51

Give other people a chance to be in charge.

You are a natural-born leader. You take charge of situations easily and have one of those personalities that just likes being the center of attention.

Most of the time, this is a good thing. Your teachers know they can put you in charge and the group will do well. Your friends know this, too. They like it when you're in charge; they like getting projects done quickly or how you can pick a game with little effort.

> "My dad says I need to let other people be the leader. But, it is really hard to let them. I get frustrated."—*Amani, age 8*

That is, most of the time!

Sometimes your friends may want to be in charge. They may want a chance to organize a project. Or pick a game. Or be first in line.

They may want—or need—to be the center of attention.

Be sensitive to this. Allow your friends a chance to shine. They deserve it as much as you do.

SUCCESS SECRET #52

Be a problem solver, not a problem maker.

Problems are going to happen in a relationship. There is no way around it. And, problems are not a bad thing. They are really just opportunities to learn new things about your friendship and a chance for the friendship to grow and become stronger.

Quiz: Are These Signs of Respect?

Directions: Circle your answer for each question.

1. Your friend has just given a presentation in class in which you noticed a lot of mistakes regarding the information they presented. Do you:
   a. Point out the mistakes during the presentation?
   b. Talk to your friend afterward and point out the mistakes?
   c. Let the teacher handle it? (It really isn't your place to correct your classmate, even if they are your friend.)

2. Your friend is having a hard day and is crying. Do you:
   a. Ignore them completely and walk away?
   b. Ask them what's wrong and insist on helping them settle down?
   c. Ask them what's wrong but step away if they ask you to give them some space?

3. Your friend just got a new outfit and wore it to school. You don't really think it looks very nice on them. Do you:
   a. Tell them it's hideous?
   b. Tell them you don't like it, but it looks okay on them?
   c. Don't say anything unless they ask, and then ask them if they like it?

4. Your friend is upset because a classmate just teased them at lunch. Do you:
   a. Tell them to get over it because it's really no big deal?
   b. Tell them to just get the kid back later?
   c. Listen to what they say and try to help them feel better?

If you mostly answered with A's, you have a lot of work to do on recognizing what is and is not respectful. Mostly B's means you are learning, but not quite there. Mostly C's means you are great at respecting other people.

Retake this quiz from time to time to check your respect know-how and make sure you are on the right track.

How you work to solve the problem is important, however. This can often determine if the friendship is going to last or if it is going to end.

There are two ways to approach most problems in a relationship: (1) You can focus on blame, who is right and who is wrong, or (2) you can focus on solving the problems. Usually, you can't do both.

Focusing on blame means all you care about is deciding who caused the problem. It doesn't get you closer to solving it. It doesn't really make you feel better over the long run. It doesn't make your relationship stronger.

Focusing on solving problems, however, does give you and your friend a chance to build a stronger friendship. When you focus on solving the problem, you have to be willing to talk to each other, listen to each other, and compromise when coming up with a solution. Problem solving requires both people to be willing to be a little wrong in order to move forward. It also requires shifting the focus away from that and being more concerned with coming up with a way to mend the relationship. Most of the time this means you have to be willing to let go of the things that hurt you and figure out how to not hurt each other in the future.

Being a problem solver means you are willing to see the situation from a different point of view. This can be really hard, too. But being willing to shift how you view things and trying to understand your friend's perspective is a great way to find solutions to almost any problem.

It's like a kaleidoscope; sometimes you need to turn things around to see another solution.

Check out the quiz "How Do You Solve Problems?"

SUCCESS SECRET **#53**

Your needs are not more or less important than your friends' needs.

We live in a big world with a lot of people. Recognizing that everyone has needs can be difficult—especially if what someone else needs is different than what you need. Let me ask you something: How can your needs be more important than someone else's?

The answer is that they can't. Not really.

Everyone's needs are equally important. The trick is to figure out how to get your needs met without hurting someone else.

Quiz: How Do You Solve Problems?

Directions: Circle your answer for each question.

1. When my friend and I disagree on something, I try my hardest to convince them why I am right.

    true   false

2. When my friend says something mean, I immediately decide they aren't my friend anymore.

    true   false

3. My friends overreact to things all of the time. When this happens, it's better to point out their mistakes and hope they don't do it again.

    true   false

4. Some problems just can't be solved.

    true   false

5. Compromise means my friend will think I'm wrong again.

    true   false

If you answered false to these questions, you are well on your way to becoming a great problem solver. Keep focusing on problem solving and avoid the blame game—these things will help you maintain your friendships.

Needs are not to be confused with wants. You may want to be first in line at the amusement park. But, this is not a need—you are probably not going to suffer a terrible fate if you aren't first. If, however, you can't wait in line because of a medical condition, then this want may become a need. In this scenario, standing in line for too long may be an impossible thing for you, and for this reason you may get to go to the front of the line. If someone got mad because you went to the front of the line in this scenario, then that would be wrong. You have a need, and the other person's want should not surpass your need.

Figuring out how to balance your needs with the needs of others requires that you first learn the difference between a need and a want. After that, it takes a lot of practice. It's hard to give up the things you want sometimes.

Once you learn to tell the difference between needs and wants, you will quickly learn that you can get your needs met and still respect the needs of others. It isn't nearly as hard as you originally thought.

Parents Sound Off

Your parents know you how easy it is to struggle with group projects, friendships, and the more social aspects of being at school. They recognize your many leadership skills and know too well how hard it is to balance that leadership with strong friendship skills.

- "(My son) hates to waste time. If a group gets stuck over tiny details that delay the group project, he jumps in to guide. That can be a problem for some with the 'I'm the boss' attitude."—*Kathleen*
- "My daughter hates being around kids that she considers immature. They really seem to annoy her, and she just has no patience for them."—*Kellie*
- "My son has to be in charge all the time. When he isn't, he complains about everything his friends are doing until they finally let him call the shots again."—*Jeff*
- "I actually worry about my daughter regarding friendships. She seems to have such a hard time fitting in. Either she is too bossy, or she goes to the other extreme and lets her friends walk all over her. There isn't any in between."—*Scott*
- "My son is a natural leader. But he uses that as a way to get what he wants from his classmates at times, and that really worries me. I want him to be a good friend, but I also realize why he does what he does."—*Rashon*

Overall, navigating the social aspects of school often means learning to compromise. Committing to learning when compromise is appropriate will help with group projects and the other sometimes difficult aspects of school.

What Do You Think?

Take a minute to ask yourself the questions on the next page. The answers will help you as you increase your social skills.

How do I show respect to my friends?

In what ways do I create problems? In what ways do I solve problems?

Can I tell the difference between things I want and things I need? Can my classmates?

Part

GIFTED AT HOME

Parents, siblings . . . nothing can make you feel more loved or bring you more frustration than your family. The burden of parental expectations and the competition you likely feel with your siblings can make things even more complicated as you try to find your footing at home.

This section goes through some of the more common challenges gifted kids may feel at home, covering things like developing good communication skills, learning to set boundaries, and handling mistakes.

But first, let's see what you think about the world of family. Remember to go through this quiz again after you've read this section. Who knows? Maybe your opinions will change!

 DOI: 10.4324/9781003232575-10

Quiz: Giftedness and Family

Directions: Circle your answer for each question.

1. Parents have higher expectations for their gifted children.

   true   *false*

2. I should try to do all of the things I am good at, even if it puts more pressure on me.

   true   *false*

3. My siblings see me as the competition for our parents' time and attention.

   true   *false*

4. Having gifted siblings is really hard—competition is inevitable.

   true   *false*

5. Mistakes at home are a sign that I am not as smart as everyone expects me to be.

   true   *false*

Chapter 7

WHY ARE YOU ALWAYS MAD AT ME?

Dealing with family can be hard at times—for anyone. Add your normal intensity to the mix, and "hard" can take on a whole new meaning. You may find yourself struggling to communicate with your parents or siblings. Dealing with family is not always easy.

> "I don't think my parents or teachers understand me, and that's hard. Really hard."—*Caleb, age 11*

Being a good communicator—knowing what to say and how to say it—is a great way to begin to smooth out any rough spots at home. Learning how to listen, speak without blaming or yelling, and accept advice can take you from constant arguments to deep, meaningful chats with your parents and siblings.

 DOI: 10.4324/9781003232575-11

SUCCESS SECRET **#54**

Listening is always more important than speaking.

Did you realize that the words "silent" and "listen" have the same letters? I like to think of it as a reminder that in order to really listen to each other, you must be silent. In that silence you can focus on what others are really saying. You can see the intent of their words through their body language and tone. You can see everything that is unspoken and hear the words that are voiced. But you can't do this if you're talking or if you're too busy thinking about your next sentence.

> "My mom says you have to be quiet in order to listen sometimes. She's right." —*Julie, age 13*

To effectively listen, you must focus purely on the person speaking.

SUCCESS SECRET **#55**

You cannot hear if you are yelling.

This secret builds on the last one. Just as you must be silent in order to hear what your parents or siblings are saying, you certainly cannot hear if you are yelling. Think of your last big argument with a family member that resulted in a yell-fest. Did either of you actually hear anything the other person said? Odds are really good you didn't. In fact, as you are remembering it now, you probably don't remember the content of that argument at all.

That's because you were so angry, so focused on getting your point across, that your mind didn't really register the words the other person was saying. The information didn't stay in your mind long enough to wind up in your memory. In addition, because your emotions were running high, you probably couldn't think straight either.

Yelling really accomplishes nothing—it doesn't enable your side of the story to be heard better, it doesn't enable you to hear the other person's side, and it doesn't allow either of you to solve the problem. All it actually accomplishes is a lot more anger, pain, and maybe even shame and guilt.

I don't know about you, but none of those emotions sound like things I want to feel often.

Check out the "Tips for Overcoming Communication Problems."

Tips for Overcoming Communication Problems

1. Remain calm. Try to keep your emotions out of the conversation.

2. Clearly state what you want.

3. If you are being asked about something you did, try to answer in a clear and honest way. Try to avoid being defensive and reacting to things.

4. Don't assume that your parents are angry unless they have said that they are angry.

5. Remember, good communication requires good listening skills. Try to listen more than you speak.

Practice these tips often. They really will help improve the communication between you and your family.

SUCCESS SECRET #56

Be willing to talk about your mistakes.

It is hard to openly discuss the poor choices you make with people, especially with your parents. You may want to deny the mistakes or pretend you didn't make them. Or, you may want to blame your behavior on something else and justify your errors somehow. None of this helps in the long run. In fact, it pretty much guarantees more problems with your parents.

> "Talk about your mistakes with family and friends. Turn them into lessons that help you improve."—*Akeem, age 13*

As we have discussed many times throughout this book, every person makes mistakes throughout their lifetime. Some of them are little, some are big, and most are not intentional. Mistakes don't define who you are—not by a long shot. What you do with the mistakes, however—how you respond—is what speaks to your character.

So, the next time your parents want to discuss some of your mistakes, don't assume they are looking to find fault with you. They are more likely just trying to help you learn from the errors that you made. They are trying to help you grow.

SUCCESS SECRET **#57**

Stay calm when discussing hard topics.

Have you ever noticed that parents really want to talk about hard things sometimes? Have you also paid attention to how you react when asked to talk about the hard stuff? Odds are you clam up, refusing to utter more than a few one-word answers to their questions. You may get angry and react to their questions by yelling. Or, you may try to leave the conversation as quickly as possible. Regardless of which reaction is most common for you, the truth is that it's very difficult to talk about certain things.

What kinds of things are hard to talk about? For some of you it could be grades or problems at school. For some, it could be risky choices you have made. For others, it may involve serious family situations like divorce. All of these topics can result in a conversation that quickly leads to heated tempers and yelling.

So, how do you stay calm when talking about the hard stuff? How do you keep your cool even when your blood is boiling? The answer lies in understanding what kinds of things make you angry to begin with, as well as a plan to stay calm when you are angry.

Remember how you can't think when you're stressed and frustrated? Well, the same thing applies to anger. Your brain doesn't make good decisions when you are angry. Staying calm by taking a break or doing some of the relaxation techniques from the first section of this book are great ways to fight back the anger and stay calm.

> "I've never actually won an argument by getting angry and yelling."—*Scott, age 12*

Keeping your cool helps you understand whatever it is your parents are saying. It also helps keep the situation from becoming explosive. The next time you find yourself getting angry when your parents start talking about your grades or another hard topic, take a deep breath and calm down. Who knows, you may discover that they only want to give you some advice you can use.

SUCCESS SECRET #58

Avoid blame.

The blame game: We're all guilty of playing it from time to time as we try to justify our behavior in some way. Maybe we say someone else did something we are guilty of doing. Maybe we blame not doing our homework on leaving stuff at school, or we say that the teacher wasn't clear about it when the truth is that we just didn't pay attention. Sometimes the blame game is used to justify problems with friends and issues with our siblings.

No matter how you use blame as a way to justify your poor choices, you need to know that blaming other people or other situations for your own behavior solves nothing.

Most of the time, your parents will know when you are choosing to blame someone or something for your own mistakes. And, most of the time, the consequence for your actions is more severe if you blame others first.

Most kids don't know when they are playing the blame game. You may not always recognize that making excuses for your behavior is a form of the blame game. For example, let's say you forgot your book at school. Saying that you were tired and forgot, or saying that a friend distracted you, are ways of blaming the action (you forgot your book) on something else (fatigue or the friend) instead of owning your behavior.

Here's the thing: Blaming others never solves a problem. Blaming others negates the truth of the hula hoop rule. You, your thoughts, and your actions are always within your control. Always.

Now, that doesn't mean you won't make mistakes. We've already established that you will. Sometimes you will forget to think through a problem before you act. Or, you won't think about the consequences for your actions. These are things that will likely happen at some point. However, saying that you are not to blame because of these things only makes the problem worse.

You are always in control of you—regardless of whether or not you remember that fact. So, the next time you are asked about something you may have done, do yourself a favor: Take responsibility for your actions and avoid the blame game completely. Check out the "Tips for Avoiding the Blame Game."

Tips for Avoiding the Blame Game

1. Always accept responsibility for your actions—even if you didn't mean to do whatever you did.

2. Remember the hula hoop trick. Don't look for loopholes that get you out of trouble. Just admit your mistakes.

3. Even if you feel out of control at times, you are still responsible for your actions. Avoid the temptation to blame your behavior on these things:
   a. "I'm tired."
   b. "I didn't understand."
   c. "I can't control my tone of voice."

4. Make a list of the things you tend to blame your behavior on. Then make a plan to avoid using those things in the future.

5. Ask your parents to partner with you on this. Develop a word or phrase they can use when they notice that you have fallen into the blame game.

Avoiding the blame game is the quickest way to take control of your own behavior and change it for the better.

SUCCESS SECRET **#59**

Accept responsibility for your actions.

As soon as you stop blaming others for your actions and recognize that you are the only one responsible for the things you do, you will begin to learn from the mistakes that you make.

Accepting responsibility, as I stated earlier, begins with the recognition that you are the only one calling the shots in your behavior. This can be a difficult thing to accept. Most of us do things to please our teachers or our parents. We don't do things only to please ourselves, and that's a good thing. It is important to understand the expectations of others and live in harmony.

That being said, living up to expectations and following rules do not give you an excuse for your behaviors. You do not get to blame what you do on the rules or on a teacher or parent's expectations. Ultimately, it is still up to you to figure things out. You choose your actions, both consciously and unconsciously. You determine the things that you do, whether you mean to or not.

Responsibility means accepting that you are in control of your actions—that you always have a choice regarding your behavior.

Take the quiz "Am I Responsible?"

SUCCESS SECRET #60

When in doubt, take a break to calm down.

It's normal to feel angry from time to time. No one is better at pushing our anger buttons than our own family. Something about being together day after day and sharing all that is most personal and intimate makes it easier to ignite one another's tempers. Add a little emotional intensity to the equation, and you have the makings for a very explosive situation.

There is a way to control it, however: Take a break before things get out of hand. The key is to recognize that you need a break, and take it before it's too late. We all have a point where all we can do is yell, a point where it is impossible to pull back from the explosion. What you need to do is figure out where your breaking point is and remove yourself from the situation before you reach it.

> "Whenever I get really mad, I have to go into my room for a while and chill. Otherwise I just yell at everyone."—*Marie, age 13*

This is often easier said than done. But, if you really utilize this success secret, you will keep yourself from blowing up and develop a habit of managing your anger.

SUCCESS SECRET #61

Celebrate moments of joy each day.

If you are going through difficult times, it may be challenging to find things to celebrate. Yet, when we look for the positive things in our lives, the

Quiz: Am I Responsible?

Directions: Circle your answer for each question.

1. When I do something I know is wrong, I own up to my mistake before my teachers or family confront me.

    true   false

2. When my parents ask me about a mistake I have made, I resist the urge to give an excuse for my behavior.

    true   false

3. My friends and teachers know that I will own my behavior, whether I've done a good thing or a not-so-good thing.

    true   false

4. My parents just found out that I received a bad grade on a test. When they confront me I say that I didn't study enough and admit my mistakes.

    true   false

5. I think it is important to own my mistakes in all situations.

    true   false

If you answered true to these questions, you are a pro at accepting responsibility for your actions. Remember that owning your mistakes is the first step toward being responsible and an important part of growing up.

---

moments to be grateful for, and the things we experience that bring us joy, we can regulate our emotions and stay in balance (Fonseca, 2017). I know it is so much easier to see what's wrong in the world and in our lives. And it is easier to think about what we need or want, instead of the many things we have. When we focus on celebrating the things we have, no matter how small, and are happy with the joys that come to most people throughout the day, we are able to shift our thinking, create a sense of calm, and improve relationships.

Use the worksheet "My Joy-Filled Moments" whenever you need help to focus on the things working in your life, instead of hyperfocusing on the things that are not working.

WORKSHEET
My Joy-Filled Moments

Directions: Take a moment to think about the different moments in your life where you were successful or times when things just seemed to "work." Then complete the worksheet below.

What Happened	How This Moment Helped Me	How I Felt About It
I remembered to make my bed before going to school.	*My mom was happy that I remembered on my own.*	*Very good!*

Parents Sound Off

Being the parents of a gifted child can be a hard job. They have to balance what they expect from you with what you need from them. It can be as confusing and frustrating for them as it is for you. Check out their words and see if you discover anything new about the things that some parents feel and say. Then, take a moment to find out how your parents feel.

- "My child is (easily) frustrated by adult-imposed boundaries at home and school."—*Tara*
- "It's hard as a parent—you don't always know when they need help or just a little motivation. Sometimes you need to push but are afraid to push too much. It gets really complicated."—*Sherrie*
- "My kids think we are always yelling at them. Sure, we are firm, but yelling? No. We don't yell."—*John*
- "Parenting my gifted children has been both my biggest joy and my biggest headache. I love all the neat ways they think. But their emotions do tend to take over the house from time to time."—*Donita*
- "Most of the time things are great with my gifted children. But when things are hard, they are extremely hard. I hate those moments." —*Tasha*

Bottom line, it's important to remember that parents want the same things you do—the ability to communicate well with you and help you when you ask.

Communication is a tricky thing. Taking the time to work through the success secrets will give you the tools you need to resist the common problems that arise between parents and kids as you approach your teen years. These tips will also give you the habits that will make those often-turbulent years much smoother.

What Do You Think?

Families can be the biggest source of comfort and pain for anyone. Take a few moments and answer the following questions for yourself to see how you feel about communicating with your parents.

What are your biggest roadblocks to communication with your parents? What can you do to reduce these roadblocks?

Everyone needs a few tricks to stay calm when talking about hard things. What are your favorite tricks?

How do you demonstrate that you have accepted responsibility for your actions? What part of being responsible do you still struggle with?

THE ART OF SAYING NO AND OTHER MYSTERIES

Balancing all of the expectations you may feel from school, your friends, parents, and yourself can be hard. Most gifted kids feel an innate obligation to share their giftedness . . . everywhere. Couple that with a keen interest in many different kinds of activities, and it is easy to see why so many gifted kids find themselves overscheduled.

> "It's hard for me to set boundaries. I usually think I can do everything—that I am supposed to do everything. I never thought of it as a choice."—*Ashlynn, age 13*

Learning about setting boundaries and how you specifically renew is crucial if you are going to learn to manage the expectations you feel from others and yourself.

 DOI: 10.4324/9781003232575-12

SUCCESS SECRET #62

Stress never solved a problem.

Stress is an interesting thing. It can be the force that drives our bodies to respond to a crisis, enabling us to escape a dangerous situation. It can also be paralyzing, making us unable to complete the simplest of things.

Stress is connected to the "fight-flight-freeze" response our bodies make in times of an emergency and is a necessary part of biology, except when it takes over our lives. Stress, taken in the extreme, can force you into that fight-flight-freeze response for too long. That is where the problems arise.

One of the biggest problems involves our brains. You see, your stress response, or that fight-flight-freeze response, is designed to slow down the part of your brain that thinks and solves problems, diverting energy to the part of your body that can get you out of the situation quickly and safely. Let's think about that for a minute: When you are stressed, you literally can't think and analyze clearly.

> "You have to put your stress aside sometimes, and just focus on getting all of your work done."—*Bishar, age 13*

Wow! No wonder it is hard to solve problems when you are stressed.

Our stress response was designed to be short term. Sadly, most of us get stuck in our stress, reliving the things that stress us out over and over and over again. Our brain reacts the same way each and every time—it slows down its thinking.

Hmm. I don't know about you, but that seems like a bad plan to me.

The best way to stop all of this? Stop stressing. Use some of the previously mention strategies for calming your brain and body. Be willing to let go of the stress and just breathe.

SUCCESS SECRET #63

Remember to take breaks.

Okay, you know you need to stop stressing about things. How do you do this? We've talked about some strategies already—things like deep breathing and taking care of yourself.

Taking breaks is another way to stop your stress cycle and enable your brain to start thinking clearly again. Although there is really no wrong way to take a break, some things can make the break more productive in terms of making sure you are releasing your stress response. Check out the "Tips for Taking Breaks the Smart Way."

SUCCESS SECRET #64

Just because you can do something, doesn't mean you have to.

Although you aren't expected to do well at everything you try, the truth is that there are a lot of things you will be very good at. You may feel that you want to do them all. What happens if you take on everything that you can excel at doing? You'll get overwhelmed.

You are going to have to learn that you can't commit to doing everything—you need to balance out the things you must do for school, with your other commitments for extracurricular activities, with the things you are expected to do at home, fitting in the things you may want to do as well. Try hard to keep everything in balance and realize that taking on too much leads to only one thing . . . more stress.

> "You need to learn to limit how much you take on. Trust me, I know. Taking on too much leads to stress." —*Maggie, age 13*

SUCCESS SECRET #65

Set good boundaries.

Part of learning to not take on too many activities at once is learning to set good boundaries for yourself. Setting boundaries relates to understanding your roles at school, at home, and in the world, as well as understanding how and when to say no to things.

Understanding your roles in the various aspects of your life is an important first step. At school, you take on the role of student. Your job in this role is

Tips for Taking Breaks the Smart Way

1. Take breaks when you feel your own stress cycle beginning—the sooner the better.

2. If you catch your stress early, try taking deep breaths or using other relaxation strategies to calm down your thoughts.

3. Go back to work as soon as you are calm. Repeat the relaxation technique each time you feel your stress rise.

4. Don't let your breaks become an excuse to not complete your work. Breaks are only to help you relax and refocus.

5. Some people control stress and pressure best when they schedule breaks into their work time. For example, plan on working for 30 minutes and then taking a 5-minute stretch break. Use a timer to keep yourself honest.

to do the best you can on your assignments and learn everything the teacher is attempting to teach. It is not your job to make sure everyone else is learning. That is the job of the teacher. Staying clear on this helps you keep from losing out on your own learning because you have been so busy helping your classmates. Now, this doesn't mean you shouldn't help, but helping to the point of neglecting your own needs doesn't demonstrate good boundaries.

At home, you are in the role of child. It is not your job to be the parent of the house or to dictate the rules. Although this may happen occasionally, observing good boundaries helps set a solid foundation for all family members.

Your role in the world is to be a good friend to others: kind, loyal, and supportive. It is not your role to parent your friends—to tell them what and how to think. That doesn't mean you can't share your ideas. You can and you should. But respecting your role as a friend means you understand the limits of that role. Your role in the world may also mean speaking out against injustice and sharing your gifts with others. It is not your role to solve all of the world's problems, however. You may feel compelled to help, and you should. Just know that many of the issues you see in the world were there before you. It took more than one person or one situation to cause the problems, and it'll take more than just you to fix them. Developing boundaries enables you to see the problems of the world and empathize with those impacted without becoming deeply distressed to the point of overwhelming yourself.

Another aspect of boundaries involves saying no to some things. This is a very hard thing for most gifted kids and adults to do. With a few tricks, learning when to say no gets easier.

Start by setting goals and clarifying what you are trying to achieve. If your goal is to get straight A's in school, then saying yes to a study party may be a good thing. If, on the other hand, you want to ace your test tomorrow, saying yes to an invitation to go to the mall when you should be studying would work against you.

In addition to setting goals and figuring out what you are hoping to achieve, you need to develop a good sense of how you function in moments of stress. All of us have a certain way we act when we are overwhelmed by things. For some, you may withdraw from everyone or get sick. For others, you may feel like you are angry all of the time. The key is figuring out what is true for you. Learn your signs that you have taken on too much and learn what to do to balance yourself back out.

SUCCESS SECRET #66

Respect the boundaries of others.

In addition to learning how to set your own boundaries and how to say no, you need to learn how to respect the boundaries of others. This can sometimes be difficult. Gifted kids are naturally adept at convincing other people to adopt their point of view. Sometimes this leads to pushing other people into situations that violate their boundaries.

It is important to learn how to respect other people's boundaries and remember that no

> "It's one thing to try to persuade someone to do what you want; it's another to bully them into doing it." —*Enrique, age 14*

really does mean no. It isn't an excuse to practice your strong verbal skills and turn the no into a yes—even if that has worked in the past.

Learning to respect other people's boundaries is a great way to help them respect yours. It also helps you learn how to balance the needs of others with your own needs. Check out the "Tips for Setting Realistic Boundaries."

Tips for Setting Realistic Boundaries

1. Begin by listing everything you are involved in and every role you have. Remember to include activities from church, sports, and any other things you are involved in. I have listed a couple things to get you started:

   a. Daughter/Son _____

   b. Student _____

   c. _____

   d. _____

   e. _____

   f. _____

2. Next to each role, list your responsibilities. For example, next to Daughter/Son, you may want to list things like following the rules, supporting my parents, and so on.

3. Rearrange the list in order of priorities: Which roles are the most important? List those first.

4. Look over the list. Can you do all of the things you have listed without exhausting yourself? Compare the list to your goals. Do they line up?

5. If you need to cut some things out, start at the bottom. Also, look over the responsibilities you've listed next to each role. Are these things that you must do? If not, see where you can adjust.

The important thing to remember is that you are not expected to do everything and be everything to everyone. You must learn to separate what is realistic for you to do from what is unreasonable.

SUCCESS SECRET **#67**

Balance, balance, balance.

We've talked a lot in this chapter about boundaries and not taking too much on at once. The key is learning to achieve balance.

Easier said than done.

Achieving balance begins with taking good care of yourself. Refer back to the previous tips about learning to relax. Make sure that you are doing the various things listed.

Additionally, it is important to understand how you renew your emotional self. Most people renew in one of two ways: alone or with others. Renewing in solitude, also known as being an introvert, means that you can get cranky when you are around people for too long. It may also mean that you prefer to be alone, reading a good book or putting together a puzzle (Sword, 2006b).

Those of you who renew through social connections, also called extroverts, often need to talk with someone in order to feel rejuvenated. You may need to retell your day just to relax. You may get stressed when you don't have people around you, even when you study or read (Fonseca, 2013).

Just like you renew in particular ways, so do the people around you. It is important to have some idea as to how they renew—this way you can learn to respect their needs as you seek to get your own met. Take the quiz "How Do I Renew?"

SUCCESS SECRET #68

Don't overcommit.

You did it: You set your goals, you learned about boundaries, and you are busy respecting other people's needs and boundaries. You have figured out how to renew each day and are in the habit of taking good care of yourself. So, how is it that you've still managed to overcommit?

There are going to be times when setting goals isn't enough to ensure that you don't take on too much. At those times you will need to learn to decide between the many important things you have on your plate. You will need to learn to limit what you get involved in.

> "Choosing between all of the things that are important to me—friends, family, my hobbies—is a struggle. But I know that when I don't make these choices, I get overwhelmed. And that's a much bigger problem."—*Elena, age 13*

It won't be fun, and you won't like some of the choices you may have to make. Sooner or later every gifted kid needs to learn how to keep from over-

Quiz: How Do I Renew?

Directions: Circle your answer for each question.

1. You come home from a busy day at school, and your mom immediately asks you how your day was. Do you:
   a. Cringe and answer as briefly as possible, hoping she'll just be quiet for a little while?
   b. Eagerly tell her all about your day, excited to share?

2. Your teacher assigns a group project at school. Do you:
   a. Ask her if you can do it alone, knowing you hate working with other kids?
   b. Look forward to sharing your ideas with another person, even though you are a little nervous about group projects?

3. It's the first day of school. Do you:
   a. Watch what the others are doing, waiting to understand the class expectations before you participate more actively?
   b. Sit down with the first group of people you see and introduce yourself?

4. You've been invited to a party with several friends. Do you:
   a. See if you can go to the party with a friend, not wanting to show up alone?
   b. Tell your friends you'll meet them there, not caring if you go alone or not?

5. Would you rather:
   a. Read a book?
   b. Play a game with a friend?

If you mostly answered with A's, you are more introverted, needing solitude to renew throughout the day. Mostly B's means you crave the attention of others in order to renew. Some of you may have struggled with answering the questions, feeling that both answers were true. In those cases, go back and pick the answer that is most often true. Most people will find themselves more introverted or more extroverted.

committing, if for no other reason than to prevent the inevitable emotional explosion that usually happens.

SUCCESS SECRET #69

Say no with grace.

A lot of kids have a hard time saying no when they are asked to do something. You may worry about how the person will react to your answer. You may also worry that they will think less of you because you aren't participating in whatever they are asking you to do. And, sometimes, you just don't say no because you don't know how.

Saying no with grace takes a little practice, especially if you need to say no to something you want to do or feel obligated to do. Begin by remembering *why* you are saying no in the first place—because you have no time or energy to take on more activities. Thank the person for thinking of you and kindly let them know that your current commitments make it impossible for you to take on another thing. If you remember to be kind and honest, the person will not feel rejected by your no.

> "I hate saying no when people ask me to do things because I hate feeling like they are going to be mad at me. I guess I just haven't learned how to say it nicely yet."—*Danielle, age 10*

Parents Sound Off

Parents know all too well how many things you tend to load on your plate. School, sports, extracurricular activities—the list is often endless. But, unlike you, they don't always see that their expectations are part of the reason you may find yourself so busy. Take a look at their quotes to help gain a fresh perspective on their opinions of the expectations and other things you may struggle to balance.

- "There is no bigger burden than having to carry others' expectations around your whole life."—*Kathleen*

- "I expect my daughter to always try her best, even when something is hard, but on the other hand, not to take herself too seriously."—*Tiare*
- "Sometimes my daughter would really just like to be like everyone else, without all the expectations. She doesn't see that most of those expectations are there because she puts them there."—*Nichole*
- "Teaching my kids how to say no to things, how to not overburden themselves with activities, has been one of the hardest things we've ever done. I still don't think we managed a very good job with it."—*James*
- "I am lousy at saying no. I think my son got it from me. But I know this is something he is just going to need to learn in order to avoid burnout later on."—*Drew*

Take a moment to talk with your parents about these things. You may discover that they expect less from you than you think.

Finding your balance is a hard thing. So is managing the expectations you feel from everyone, including yourself. Review the tips in this chapter and the questions in the following section often. The better you are at living a balanced life, the more you will be able to accomplish in the long run, and the better you will feel.

What Do You Think?

Setting good boundaries and balancing expectations can be a difficult thing for gifted kids to learn. Think about the success secrets you've read and look at the following questions. Answering them will give you insight regarding your own feelings about expectations and setting good boundaries.

Being honest with yourself, do you think you sometimes take on too much . . . too little? Is it a problem for you?

What do you need to renew each day and stay in balance? What are the biggest barriers to achieving this?

It can be hard to maintain good boundaries with friends and family. Do you consider yourself good at setting and maintaining boundaries, or is this something that is hard for you?

Chapter 9

STOP TRYING TO FIX ME, I'M NOT BROKEN

Your parents give you advice all of the time. Your teachers are constantly sharing a better way of doing things. Heck, even this book is giving you secrets to success. Everyone seems to be giving you some advice on how to be you, almost as if you aren't enough as you are.

At least, that's how it may seem to you.

Advice is not a bad thing. Receiving advice does not mean that the person giving it thinks you are somehow wrong or damaged. Usually the advice is given out of kindness, as a way to help you see a different way of doing something. Learning how to give and receive advice is a great way to improve your relationships at home, as well as become a stronger individual.

> "I hate it when people assume things about me because I'm smart. I wish they'd just stop and get to know me first—the real me." —*Jin, age 9*

DOI: 10.4324/9781003232575-13

SUCCESS SECRET #70

You have allies.

Just like siblings and extended family members are your cheerleaders, your parents are often your best allies. So are other trusted adults in your life.

> "If I can remember that my parents are trying to help, I don't get as mad."—*Ellie, age 10*

They are there to guide you and help you navigate through the difficult journey of growing up. They can be your partners and support group.

Like in any partnership, there are times when you are going to get frustrated with them. Maybe you don't see eye to eye with their rules or their advice. Maybe it feels like they are trying to stop you from growing up at times. And, maybe they are in some ways.

But your parents and other trusted adults are your allies in the long run. Much of the advice they offer and the rules they impose serve a purpose you can't really see or understand when you are young. Appreciate your allies and all of the ways they try to guide you. If their advice doesn't seem to work, talk with them. Ask questions and work together. After all, a healthy partnership is not a one-sided deal.

SUCCESS SECRET #71

Making a mistake is not the end of the world.

One of the more common reasons kids and their parents get into arguments has to do with mistakes. Often a child will break a family rule or make a mistake at school. The parent will then talk with the child to try to determine what happened. Eventually that conversation leads to consequences of some form and a lot of hurt feelings on both sides (especially as you get older and you get better at making your parents feel guilty).

Your parents know that you are going to make mistakes during your childhood—they expect it. And, as we've discussed many times already, you should expect that you will make a few mistakes as well. What gets you into trouble isn't just the mistake; it's the way the mistake is handled.

Did you admit the error, or did you fall into the blame game trap we've discussed in earlier chapters? Were you willing to talk about the mistake calmly, or did you yell and argue? Did you try to learn from the situation, or did you refuse to accept responsibility for your actions? All of these things determine how your parents will react to the mistake made.

No matter how things go, no matter if you react in a way that makes the mistakes worse, it is still not the end of the world. Let me repeat that: Making a mistake is not the end of the world. It's only a mistake, a chance to learn something new and try again. Check out the "Tips if You Make a Mistake."

SUCCESS SECRET **#72**

Admit your mistakes.

Although making mistakes is a normal part of growing up, it doesn't mean you aren't obligated to deal with the error and the consequences of the error in some way.

As I mentioned earlier, most of the problems that come from poor choices happen as a result of how you chose to deal with your own behavior. Pretending the mistake didn't happen, or worse, lying about it, only makes things worse between you and your parents. It creates an even bigger problem.

There are many reasons you may want to lie or blame someone else for your mistakes. I talked about some of the reasons when I reviewed the blame game—things like avoiding the consequence or avoiding feeling like you failed at something. Most of the time, you just avoid taking ownership for your choices and behaviors because it's hard. You may think that admitting your error makes you a disappointment in the eyes of your parents, teachers, friends,

> "I really struggle when it comes to admitting my mistakes. I don't know, it just always feels like when I admit a mistake it means I am not gifted, not perfect. I hate feeling like I am not perfect."—*Ami Jane, age 12*

or other allies. Maybe you feel like the mistake confirms that you aren't worthy of your parents' trust and love. Or, maybe you're just really afraid of being in trouble.

Tips if You Make a Mistake

1. First and foremost, you must admit the mistake.

2. Make apologies or anything else you need to do to demonstrate your ownership of the mistake.

3. Ask yourself why you made the mistake. Did you forget something (like writing down an assignment) or did you just not think about the rules? Be as honest as you can on this.

4. Come up with a plan to avoid making the same mistake again. If you forgot something at school, how can you keep yourself from forgetting again?

5. If the mistake caused a second problem, do you need to address that problem also? For example, if forgetting your assignment at school caused you to fail a class, what must you do to address that failure now?

Everyone makes mistakes from time to time. It is important to look at these mistakes not as failures, but as opportunities to learn and grow. What can you learn from the mistake you made?

The truth is that mistakes themselves have no bearing on your worth. As we have already said, what you choose to do with the mistake—how you choose to respond—demonstrates more about you than the error you've made.

So, now you're convinced that you must admit your mistakes in order to move forward. But, how? Yes, you must take responsibility as we've discussed earlier in this section. Sometimes that can be tricky. Gifted kids are very good at fooling people, especially themselves. It would be easy for you to convince yourself that the situation really isn't your fault or that the mistake isn't that bad at all. It's hard to be objective about your own behavior and even harder to tell when you aren't. Hard or not, however, admitting your mistakes is the only way to give yourself an opportunity to learn from them and avoid repeating the same mistakes in the future.

SUCCESS SECRET #73

Make amends for your mistakes.

The next step in dealing with mistakes is making amends. This means not only admitting the problem, which you have already done, but also taking responsible for the impact of the mistake and dealing with the consequences.

Let's say you cheated on a test and got caught. The first thing you have to do is admit that you did it. Then you need to find a way to make amends. In my house, that would entail an apology to the teacher, as the act of cheating is a sign of disrespect. In your house, it could be something different.

What you do to make amends isn't as important as actually doing it. Find a way to make up for the mistake, to fix any harm that was created by the mistake. Then do it. Talk with your parents and the person you wronged. See how you can fix the problem.

There will be times when you can't fix things. This is particularly true if the error you made resulted in someone else being hurt physically or emotionally. But there is always a way you can make amends, even if it doesn't fix the problem. Read the "Tips for Making Amends."

One of the hardest things about mistakes and making amends is the tendency to define yourself by your mistakes. Avoid this trap as much as possible and remember that everyone makes mistakes. Taking the time to make amends for your mistakes is one of the best ways to show your responsibility and willingness to learn.

SUCCESS SECRET #74

Seek reconciliation.

Reconciliation, or finding harmony, is the last step in moving forward after making a big mistake. It follows admitting the problem and making amends and involves seeking forgiveness, typically through an apology.

Although this step may seem simple, forgiveness isn't something you can control. Sure, you can admit what you have done, apologize for your actions, and find a way to make amends. But, doing all of that does not necessarily mean the person you wronged will forgive you. That choice is completely up to them. Just as it is your choice to decide how you will act and feel in a variety of situations, everyone has a similar choice.

Tips for Making Amends

1. First admit the mistake to the person you wronged.

2. Ask that person if there is a way you can "make things right."

3. If there is a way to make things right, be sure to do it quickly and without complaint.

4. Make a plan to avoid making the same poor choice in the future.

5. Let it go. Don't define yourself and your self-worth by the mistake you have made.

There will be times when a mistake isn't forgiven, when something you have done can't be fixed with an apology. In those situations, you have to figure out how to release your own guilt and move forward.

For gifted kids this can be really tough. As with many things, you tend to feel guilt very deeply. As a result, you may struggle to let go of a mistake when someone isn't accepting your apology. You may try over and over to convince the person to forgive you.

And it may not work. At all. That is the other person's choice, just as it was yours to ask for his forgiveness.

If a friend chooses *not* to forgive you after a mistake, you have to let it go. You have done what is required of you—you accepted your part of the problem. You tried to make amends. And you sought reconciliation. There is nothing else you can do in the situation. So stop twisting yourself into a mess to make your friend forgive you. Learn to let it go.

> "I really have a hard time when a friend can't forgive me. It always makes me feel like I have done some horrible, horrible thing. I need to try to remember that even if someone doesn't forgive you for something you've done, it doesn't mean you can't forgive yourself." —*Akira, age 9*

SUCCESS SECRET #75

No one is ever really alone.

As a gifted kid, you know what it feels like to be alone at times. You know that not everyone gets you all of the time. You know you think differently than most of the people you know. You know that you are pretty unique. But this doesn't mean you are alone.

No one is as alone as they feel at times. There are always people around that you can lean on, even if you've never leaned on them before. The problem is, you seldom remember who all of the members of your support team are when you are in the middle of a crisis. As a result, you may feel very lonely even though there are people in your life to help you.

Take a minute to think about all of the people you can turn to when you need support. Think of your family, your friends, and even your teachers. Take a few minutes and complete the worksheet "My Support Team." It will help you remember that you are not alone.

SUCCESS SECRET #76

Lean on each other when things are hard.

Human beings are social creatures. Even if you renew through solitude, you still need people in your life: a support team. The previous success secret gave you a chance to discover all of the different members of your support team. It also gave you a chance to remember all of the reasons they are important to you. But, none of that matters if you forget to lean on them when things are hard.

> "My family makes getting through the stress so much easier."—*Nona, age 9*

Maybe you were taught that you should stand on your own two feet all of the time. Maybe you think leaning on your friends and family makes you weak. The truth is that we all need someone to turn to from time to time.

Life can be hard, especially when you're gifted. Sometimes your own intensities may get the better of you. Having friends and family to lean on makes the journey a little easier.

WORKSHEET
My Support Team

1. Draw a small circle in the space below. Inside the circle write your name.

2. Make a larger circle around the first one and list the members of your family who support you.

3. Add another circle and list your extended family. This can include uncles and aunts, grandparents, and any other members of your extended family who support you and your endeavors.

4. Add more circles that include friends, teachers, and other people who support you.

5. Decorate your picture of concentric circles with things that have meaning to you.

Keep this picture someplace where it can remind you of all of the people who are part of your support team. As time passes, you will want to redo the list. Refer back to it any time you feel in need of a little more support.

SUCCESS SECRET #77

Take it easy on yourself.

I don't know about you, but most of the gifted kids I've talked to are really hard on themselves. They demand perfection and precision in all tasks. When they make a mistake or earn a grade lower than they want, they work even harder the next time. They are driven and intense in all aspects of their lives.

And, they never ease up.

Approaching life that way is not necessarily a bad thing. Anything taken to extremes can be too hard to manage. Putting constant pressure on yourself will throw you into an emotional cycle that can be very hard to break. Remember, you aren't just intense when it comes to academic performance. You are passionate in all aspects of your life, especially when it comes to your feelings.

> "You're going to make mistakes sometimes. When that happens, try to learn from it—don't beat yourself up. That never helps anything."—*Sydney, age 13*

Learning to give yourself permission to make a mistake, to fail, is the first step in learning to control the impact of the pressure you put on yourself. It is the key to everything else. So the next time you are mentally beating yourself up for making a mistake or failing at something, try to remember that the mistake really doesn't define you as a person.

It is just a mistake, an opportunity to learn and try again.

Parents Sound Off

Parents know how important a strong family unit can be, and they struggle with how their kids interact with each other. Take a look at the following quotes and talk with your parents about their feelings. You may learn something new.

- "(My child's) sister is one of the few that she lets herself be silly with."—*Cho*
- "(My kids) have been each other's best friends and partners in crime since childhood. I'm glad they have each other."—*Jennifer*

- "My daughter is so hard on herself, even when we remind her that she needs to relax. I think it just goes with the territory."—*Lien*
- "When push comes to shove, my kids know I'll always be their biggest fan. Of course, that doesn't keep them from driving me insane from time to time."—*Kristine*
- "Seeing my son feel so guilty every time he makes a mistake or has a fight with friends is so painful for me to watch. I just wish he felt more connected with others."—*Shu*

Remember, no one really understands you like your allies, especially those at home. And although there may be conflict, learning to respect and lean on each other can set you up for lifelong relationships you will treasure.

Being accepted in one's family is something every child has a right to experience. Sadly, however, this doesn't always happen. Read through the tips in this chapter and reflect on the following questions as you look at how you are connected to those most important in your life. And, if you struggle to connect with your family, look for ways to connect with others who can support you as you go from being a child to an adult.

What Do You Think?

Feeling accepted in your family is something every child needs and wants. Take some time to think about the following questions and determine the ways in which you feel connected.

How do you know that you are accepted in your family or with your friends? Are there other adults you feel connected to? Who are they?

When you do something hurtful, how do you make amends and move forward?

If a friend wasn't feeling connect to their family, what advice would you give them to improve the situation?

GIFTED IN THE WORLD

You aren't only gifted at home and at school. Your giftedness impacts every aspect of who you are and every setting you are in. Understanding the ways your giftedness impacts your interactions in the world and how to maximize your potential and happiness is essential to your overall well-being.

This section covers the many ways you can embrace everything it means to be gifted and increase your life satisfaction while sharing your many gifts with the world. Review the various success secrets, tips, and worksheets while thinking about how you may want to impact the greater good of the planet.

But first, let's see what you think about bringing your giftedness into the world. Remember to go through this quiz again after you've read this section or anytime you want to reevaluate the ways your gifts make it into the world.

 DOI: 10.4324/9781003232575-14

Quiz: Gifted in the World

Directions: Circle your answer for each question.

1. I must try to do everything I am interested in—it is the only way to show my giftedness.

    true   false

2. Being gifted means I have to help everyone.

    true   false

3. The needs of others are more important than my own needs.

    true   false

4. If I don't share my gifts, then I am just being selfish.

    true   false

5. I should hide my gifts at times so that I don't seem like I am bragging or putting others down.

    true   false

NORMAL OR AUTHENTIC

Normal—it's such a loaded word. Commonly defined as the usual or ordinary, most of us strive to be "normal," which makes sense. We are hardwired to connect. Being normal, we often think, increases our ability to connect. Connections, in turn, increase our happiness, make us feel more safe, and give meaning to our lives.

> "There really is no such thing as normal."—*Kane, age 12*

What is normal, really?

I believe there is no such thing as normal. There is "expected" and "typical." But normal—yeah, that is a myth.

Instead of striving for normal, why not aim for authenticity? When you are being authentic, you are being true to yourself and acting consistently with who you are inside. You are true to your strengths, your values, and your gifts. You own your faults and strive to correct errors when you make them.

 DOI: 10.4324/9781003232575-15

When you are being authentic, genuine relationships come more naturally. Authenticity, it appears, is far more essential than the myth of normal.

The next success secrets cover the ideas of acceptance, identifying your feelings, and knowing your "why"—all contributors to living an authentic life.

SUCCESS SECRET **#78**

Accept yourself as you are.

You are an amazing person. You are intelligent and have an almost innate need to learn. You love to throw yourself into the most difficult of projects, but you misspell the simplest of words in your essays. You are both serious and concerned about the world, yet you also find the time to laugh and have fun. You can move from happy to sad so fast it throws you off balance. And, you care deeply about everything.

It can be hard to accept all of these aspects of yourself at times. You may find yourself focusing on the parts of you that you struggle with, things like rigid thinking, or your constant doubt about your giftedness. You may have a hard time seeing your natural intensities as a good thing.

Accepting yourself, however, means recognizing those parts you don't like as well. It means looking for positive ways to think about your difficulties. For example, your rigid thinking can be turned into perseverance, your doubts can be turned into self-reflection, and your intensity can be turned into passion. All of these are admirable qualities. Although you may struggle with how you deal with some of these things, the qualities themselves are a great part of who you are. Try completing the worksheet "My Strengths."

SUCCESS SECRET **#79**

Accept others as they are.

Once you've figured out how to accept yourself as you are, you need to find a way to accept others as well. This can be tricky. You will often see others' potential, getting more and more frustrated when they don't live up it.

WORKSHEET
My Strengths

1. List at least three things you consider strengths. Your list could include things like "I do my chores without being asked" or "When I make a promise, I keep it." Be sure to include things that relate to school, friends, and family.

2. List at least three things about yourself that frustrate you. It could be things like "I take too long to do homework" or "I sometimes yell at my friends."

3. Look at your list from Step #2. Can you turn any of those things into a positive quality? For example, with "I take too long to do my homework," can you rephrase that to be a strength? ("I am persistent with my work and strive for my best.")

4. Remember that most of our weaknesses are strengths that we aren't managing well. Focus on the positive.

5. Brainstorm ways to improve the weaknesses you feel you have. If you take too long on your homework, look at the positive attributes of that and then figure out how to manage it better. For example, you know that taking a long time is positive in that it shows your persistence. Manage it better by learning to let go of some things or using tools like a timer to help you stay on track.

6. Read your list of positive attributes every time you find yourself getting down about you.

Rewrite this list often, as your opinions about your strengths and weaknesses will change over time. The important thing to remember is that within every weakness is a strength we aren't really recognizing.

Sometimes you will see the negative things your friends do as personality flaws, instead of viewing them as behaviors that can change. You may forget that we are all just works in progress, changing and developing over time.

Accepting others is necessary for you to develop both empathy (the ability to feel what someone else is feeling) and compassion (the desire to help someone when they are hurting). Building empathy and compassion will help you build your emotional intelligence.

So, first accept yourself—flaws and all. Then, accept your friends. The empathy and compassion you develop along the way will help you in ways you may not realize until you are much older. Check out the "Tips for Learning to Accept Others."

SUCCESS SECRET **#80**

Don't live to the labels.

Sometimes we have a hard time accepting ourselves and others because of the way we have labeled things. You may think you can't like the cheerleader in your class because she is not supposed to be smart or accepting of the smart kids. Or maybe you think that being gifted means you are a nerd, something you are avoiding, so you refuse to think of yourself as gifted because you refuse to believe you are a nerd.

Labels don't really define people, and stereotypes are just that . . . stereotypes. People are often characterized in a certain way because of a certain label, without any regard for who they may actually be.

Labels are around to serve one purpose and one purpose only. They help provide an umbrella of meaning for a specific set of things or people. For example, we label the things we put food on as dishes. Some dishes are made of plastic, some of paper, and still others of clay. They come in a variety of shapes, sizes, and colors, and they serve a variety of purposes. But we still call all of them dishes.

> "Never think that because you're smart, you are a nerd. You are whoever you want to be."—*Kyle, age 9*

If we were to assume that dishes only meant a specific type, or size, or shape of dish, we would be wrong—we would be accepting a stereotype.

Tips for Learning to Accept Others

1. Think about a person you struggle with—someone who really drives you nuts.

2. Focus on the behavior that bothers you, not the person.

3. Write down the things about the behavior that frustrate you.

4. Try to see things through the other person's point of view. Can you understand why they behave the way they do?

5. Try not to judge the other person's behavior. If you are frustrated and can't get past it, talk with them. See if you can work it out. If not, let it go. And remember, it is the behavior that annoys you, not the person.

Accepting others, flaws and all, is something that takes some work to master. As you learn this skill, you will find that accepting yourself will also become easier.

The same is true about the labels we give to each other. Knowing that you are gifted serves the purpose of telling you about certain ways you may be behaving. Assuming that because you are gifted you must be a nerd, you'll only have a few friends, or you're always right would be wrong. You may or may not like the same things as other gifted people in your class.

Never succumb to labels and stereotypes. Instead, take time to figure out who you are on the inside, and do the same with your friends.

SUCCESS SECRET #81

No one likes having their flaws pointed out.

Yes, you do know and see a lot more than the average person. You notice inconsistencies and errors in the world around you. You definitely notice when a friend tells a story wrong, or a

> "I used to tell people when they were making mistakes on things. I stopped when my friends started getting really mad."—*Cassidy, age 9*

teacher misspells a word, or your mom tells your dad something different from what she told a friend on the phone.

You notice it all.

Noticing everything does not mean you should point it all out. As we have said before, people are flawed. That's just the way it is. They make mistakes, they say the wrong things, and sometimes they even lie. Most of the time they don't mean to do these things; it just happens.

And, you know what?

It happens to you as well. There are times when you make mistakes, right? You say the wrong things sometimes, don't you? And maybe you even tell the occasional lie.

If someone was around to constantly point out these things, do you think you would feel better or worse about things? Yep, that's right—you'd feel worse. Guess what? That's probably how your friends are feeling every time their flaws are pointed out to them.

Think about this before you point out a mistake. Ask yourself if it will help your friend or hurt them. Ask yourself if it is information they need. Sometimes you will decide that it is. Most of the time you'll realize that pointing out their mistakes is not as important as you thought.

SUCCESS SECRET **#82**

Redefine normal for yourself.

We've talked a lot about normalcy, acceptance, and tolerance over the past few pages. Really, the whole conversation boils down to this: You are the one who needs to define "normal" for yourself.

Yes, your parents, teachers, and friends will influence your ideas. In the end, it is you who will make decisions regarding acceptance. It is you who will decide what is right and what is wrong. You control your thoughts.

> "Stand up for what you believe in, even if it means you are the only one standing."—*Meghan, age 13*

Will you learn to embrace others' differences and unique qualities? Will you be gentle to yourself and your friends? Will you stand against bullies and take the harder road from time to time?

It takes a strong heart to accept things that are different, and an even stronger heart to defend those in need. In the end, we all live on this planet together—and we all need to find a way to get along.

SUCCESS SECRET **#83**

When in doubt, know what you feel.

Life can feel very confusing at times. You may think one thing, feel something else, and behave in another way altogether. Or at least, that is how it seems. The truth is that there is a connection between your deepest internal thoughts, feelings, and actions. When you feel like your thoughts, feelings, and actions are all disconnected, it is important to dig deeper. Perhaps that big brain is lying to you. Or maybe you are out of touch with your feelings. Or you are not being authentic in your actions. Pulling everything into consistent alignment is essential to living an authentic life.

Start with looking at your emotions. What are you really feeling at this moment? If it doesn't match your behavior or your thoughts, it's time to look more closely. Sometimes knowing your feelings is tricky. Increasing your emotional vocabulary is a great way to get more detailed about what you are feeling and do a better job living authentically. Create an emotion wheel for yourself to help you build your emotional literacy (see the worksheet "My Emotions Wheel"). Update it every few months as you learn and grow.

SUCCESS SECRET **#84**

Recognize your authenticity.

Throughout this chapter, we've talked about living consistently with who you are—living authentically. Sometimes this is easier said than done. To live from a place of acceptance and authenticity, you must recognize when you are consistent in thought, feeling, and action, versus those times when you are not. You must also understand

> "I hate it when people say things just to fit in. It is so much more important, I think, to just be who you are."—*Geoff, age 12*

WORKSHEET
My Emotions Wheel

Directions: Look at the completed emotion wheel below. Circle those emotions that best represent what you feel. Now create your own emotion wheel. Put in all the different types of feelings you have. Use the completed wheel as a guide.

Note. Adapted from Fonseca, 2020.

when you need to regulate your emotions and your thinking to manage your behavior. Both skills are vital if you are going to live authentically without upsetting everyone around you.

But where should you start?

Start with noticing those moments when you are thinking-feeling-acting in a way that seems like the real you. Separate those moments from the times when you are just trying to please people. What do you notice about the differences between these times? The more you pay attention to how you are acting at different times and with different people, the sooner you will be able to live in a place of alignment. Yes, there will be times when you must manage your behavior and not express the full intensity of your emotions. But this shouldn't mean that you can't still be authentic. The key is remembering that how you think, feel, and act are all up to you—you are the only thing in your hula hoop!

SUCCESS SECRET #85

Know your "why."

Simon Sinek, a highly recognized speaker and author, is famous for talking about your "why." His book, *Start With Why: How Great Leaders Inspire Everyone to Take Action*, is a staple among new leaders in almost every field of business and study (Sinek, 2009). According to Sinek, your personal "why" is your purpose. Everything you do relates back to your purpose. Discovering your why can help you find your motivation, live authentically, and experience more satisfaction with your life.

To help you determine your current purpose in life, I want you to review some of the things you've discovered about yourself already: your giftedness traits, your strengths, your intensities, and your values. From the different qualities you've already learned about yourself, take a moment and craft your *why* statement, something I call your life motto.

Some examples of life mottos created by gifted children just like you during my live workshops include the following:

- Be like a boat—stay afloat.
- Explore diversity.
- Live bravely and be kind.
- Love human, think past humanity.
- Creative writing is my strength and power.

Now it's your turn: Take a moment to complete the worksheet "My Life Motto," and write your tagline. Refer to it whenever you are making a tough decision or checking to see if you live from your purpose.

Parents Sound Off

Parents really understand your unique qualities and how being unique is both a good thing and something you may be struggling with. Check out their thoughts in the following quotes. Any surprises?

- "My two children are in a gifted class at their school. They have told me that they like it a lot because their classmates understand them for the first time. Now, everything they say and do feels normal. I've never seen them so happy."—*Bette*
- "My daughter struggles to relate to most of her peers. She is not interested in the latest fashions and fads, which makes it hard for her to jump into a conversation with other (kids)"—*Tiare*
- "My son is a rebel. He really doesn't care what other people think. He does his own thing and seems perfectly happy that way."—*Steve*
- "My daughter used to struggle making friends, and she couldn't understand why people seemed so mean all of the time. That changed as she got older and began to understand their points of view a bit more."—*Judi*
- "I just love that my kid is so connected with the world and what's happening. He just told me that he wants to be a doctor to help the world deal with large-scale pandemics. What a great way to deal with everything that has been happening."—*Eric*

Understanding your parents' perspective on you and your unique qualities is a great way to broaden your thoughts. Take some time to talk with them about all of their feelings, and be sure to share your points of view as well.

Learning to embrace your unique qualities and think for yourself can be a challenge at any age, but especially as you enter your preteen and teen years. Review this section as often as you need to in order to remind yourself how to stay true to your own thoughts about yourself and the world.

WORKSHEET
My Life Motto

Directions: List your giftedness attributes, characters strengths, and values in the columns below. Then write a sentence that defines you or your life motto. Use the examples in the book as a reference.

Gifted Attributes	Character Strengths	Values

My Life Motto: _____

_____

_____

_____

_____

What Do You Think?

Now it's your turn. Really think about what it means to accept yourself and your friends. Take a few minutes to ask yourself the following questions and see how you can remember to live authentically.

Do you accept yourself as you are? How do you show this?

Do you accept your friends as they are? How do you show this?

How can you live in alignment with your "why"?

SHARING MY GIFTS

One of the most interesting things I have learned from the focus groups with thousands of gifted children across the world is how much gifted children care about the world and want to share their gifts in order to help. I am not surprised. As a gifted child, I was very much the same. I dreamed of saving the planet from pollution like a superhero. Or rescuing people who were enslaved and marginalized. I just couldn't understand why some of the unfair and cruel things that happen in the world were happening. It still bothers me.

> "I have a real problem with overscheduling. There are just too many things I want to do. And, of course, I always want to do them perfectly."—*Lizbeth, age 14*

In this chapter, you will learn ways to harness your deep thoughts about world events with action. The success secrets will also help you learn to cultivate your empathy, set goals, and practice a little self-care when needed.

 DOI: 10.4324/9781003232575-16

SUCCESS SECRET **#86**

Discover your passions.

As a gifted adult, I live an intense life. I have many interests and passions. My guess is that you do, too. You likely have so many things you are interested in that you may get overwhelmed. You may enjoy robotics, engineering, making cupcakes, music, learning languages, art, and world events. It's enough to exhaust you.

Or, maybe you haven't really figured out what you are passionate about yet. That's where this success secret comes in. Discovering the things you care about, something you want to do, or causes you wish to support is an essential aspect of getting to know yourself as a gifted human. When you cultivate a life filled with your passion projects, you will feel more satisfied. Check out the worksheet "Things I Care About."

SUCCESS SECRET **#87**

Learn how to become more empathetic.

We live in a diverse world, filled with billions of other humans. We will understand some of them. Others, we will not. That doesn't mean we can't learn to understand them. Beyond understanding, we can also learn to be compassionate to their needs. This type of "feeling" what another feels is called empathy.

Empathy is an emotional skill that develops over time. It is complicated enough that I have written entire books about it. For this book, I just want you to know that empathy with others is vital if you are going to live a passion and purpose-filled life. Empathy and compassion enable you to recognize the needs of others. It is this skill that helps you realize when someone needs your support. And it is empathy that allows you to take action when it is required.

For many gifted children, empathy comes naturally. That said, it often causes a lot of emotional distress as you take on others' emotions without first learning how to differentiate someone else's thoughts and feelings from your own. This last part—developing emotional boundaries between yourself and others—is necessary to establish healthy empathy.

WORKSHEET
Things I Care About

Directions: Make a list of your passion areas in the first column. Then complete the rest of the worksheet.

Passion Area	Why I Like It	Similar Areas I Might Want to Learn About	What I Can Do to Help or Support
The environment	Without taking care of the planet, we will destroy it	Deforestation, melting polar ice caps, the dying coral reefs, how to conserve	Teach my family about conservation.

The "Tips for Building Empathy" can help you enhance your natural feelings of empathy and ensure a healthy expression of the skill.

SUCCESS SECRET **#88**

Embrace diversity.

We live in a wonderfully diverse world, with many different cultural traditions, languages, and even appearances. These differences paint a beautiful picture. When we embrace the diversity of the world, we begin to see the value of the differences. If we dig deeper, we can also learn that we are more alike than we are different. As humans, we all have a need to belong, a need to be seen and heard, and a need to feel safe. This is something that unites us. And our differences just make everything so much more interesting.

> "I love how different everyone is in the world. Different looks. Different traditions. Different experiences. It makes the world interesting."—*Mason, age 10*

Embrace both the similarities and diversity in this world. You will grow your world view and have more ways to share your gifts with the planet.

SUCCESS SECRET **#89**

Explore things that interest you.

We live in a big world filled with an endless array of things we can learn and do. Even more exciting is recognizing that living in a digital information age means we have access to more knowledge than we ever have previously. You can learn nearly anything. So, take some time to learn new things. Figure out what is important to you—what causes or events have meaning to you. Then figure out what you can do to share your gifts with the world. If you have access to information, do some research.

> "There are so many things I find interesting in the world. And I want to do them all."—*Joshua, age 12*

Tips for Building Empathy

The following tips will help you to develop stronger levels of empathy:

- Identify the feelings in yourself and others.
- Place no judgments on others' feelings or opinions.
- Ask how someone feels.
- Ask if you can help (i.e., "Is there anything I can do?" "What do you need?").
- Offer kindness and support (i.e., "I know it was a hard day. I'm here if you need anything.").
- Resist the urge to "fix" the other person. Being empathetic means feeling another's feelings and understanding them without trying to fix the issue.

Note. Adapted from Fonseca, 2019.

If you can't find the information you are looking for, ask a parent, teacher, or other trusted adult to help.

It is an exciting time in which we are limited mostly by our imaginations. Cultivate your curiosity and discover something new and interesting.

SUCCESS SECRET #90

Plan ahead or go behind.

My grandmother was a force. She created new industries and kept her family safe and secure during the Great Depression—all at a time when women weren't supposed to do these things. She always said a person must "plan ahead or go behind." It is a phrase I grew up with from my earliest memories. And one I share with all of you.

Planning ahead refers to goal setting. Just as you should cultivate your interests and pursue things that excite you, you should also practice goal setting to learn how to take action on your dreams. It isn't enough to be aspirational. You must learn how to set goals, make plans, and take action if you want to achieve the different things you want.

Use the worksheet "My Goals" to practice setting goals. The more you both set and attain goals, the more you begin to harness Grandma's statement "plan ahead or go behind."

SUCCESS SECRET **#91**

Let go and learn to just "be."

Sharing your gifts with the world can be exhausting over time. You may loosen your boundaries and become distressed by other emotions. Or you may overcommit, only to leave yourself too tired and mentally drained to do your best work. This time of overwhelm is not uncommon with gifted children. Learning to let go and be present at the moment, with no worries about the past or the future, is a great way to develop self-care and balance.

"Mindfulness," another word for being present in the moment, involves training your brain to just experience this present moment fully. It means that your mind, your feelings, and your body are all focused on the same thing. If you are eating a strawberry, for example, mindfulness means you are only experiencing the strawberry—how it tastes, smell, looks. Nothing else matters at that moment.

Look at the "Tips for Being Mindful" and practice a couple of strategies. The more you can train yourself to be fully aware of the moment, the more you can take on your passions and share your gifts without becoming overwhelmed.

SUCCESS SECRET **#92**

Become response-able.

Speaking of becoming overwhelmed, have you ever noticed that you can't respond to others' needs or give of yourself when you are completely drained? There is just nothing left to give. This can happen on creative projects, schoolwork, and anything that requires sustained effort or attention. It is essential to take care of yourself and your needs regularly to have enough mental and emotional stamina to complete the things you want.

WORKSHEET
My Goals

Directions: Take a moment to think about the things you want to accomplish. Then write a goal that allows you to accomplish the task. Include the potential barriers and benefits you will experience when you achieve the goal.

Goal	Potential Barriers	Benefits to Completing Goal
I want to learn how to speak Chinese.	■ *I might not have time* ■ *It could be very hard to learn a foreign language* ■ *I might get bored with it quickly* ■ *I may not have anyone to practice speaking with*	■ *I will be bilingual* ■ *It could help me in the future*

Tips for Being Mindful

Here are a few tips to develop and strengthen mindfulness:

- **Mindful Breathing:** Close your eyes and take a deep, slow breath through your nose. Hold briefly and exhale through your mouth. Continue with this pattern of breathing as you focus only on the breath moving through your body. As thoughts float into your mind, allow them to pass without giving them your attention. Continue for several minutes.

- **Mindful Eating:** Select an item to eat, like a strawberry or piece of banana. Take a moment to notice the color, smell, and texture of your food. As you take a bite, focus fully on the experience. What do you taste? What do you smell? Slowly chew your food, noticing the way it feels in your mouth and as you swallow. Notice how the food makes you feel, the sensations as it moves through your body. Continue until you are finished with your food.

- **Mindful Walking:** Take a morning walk or hike. Focus fully on the act of walking. How does your body feel as it moves through the space? What does the air smell like? How does the wind or sun feel? Breathe deeply as you continue your walk, focusing only on the act of walking. As other thoughts come to mind, allow them to move gently through you without paying attention to them. Continue in this manner until your walk is complete.

- **Mindful Moments:** Take a moment and find a place where you can be quiet for a few minutes. I will often use my office, my car (while not driving, of course), or even the bathroom. Close your eyes and inhale a few deep breaths. Focus on your body. Where are you feeling tension? Concentrate your focus on those areas, imagining your body releasing the tightness in your muscles and fully relaxing. Do this with each area of tension until you feel fully relaxed. As thoughts float into your mind, release them without paying undue attention to them. Continue for a minute or so until your mind is clear and your body is relaxed.

Note. Adapted from Fonseca, 2019.

This idea of having mental and emotional stamina is something I like to call being "response-able." When you can respond to your creative endeavors, to a crisis, or to a request from a teacher, family member, or friend, it means that your brain is calm enough to engage. You have the energy needed to complete what you are asked to do. You have the emotional regulation necessary to successfully obtain your goal. You are response-able.

Sometimes it is hard to recognize when you can respond to the needs of others or yourself. That is where the worksheet "I'm Response-able When . . ." can help. Take a moment to reflect on the times when you were able to efficiently complete tasks, help others, or respond to someone's needs. How did you feel? What can you notice about your thoughts, feelings, or actions? Make a list of the signs that you were is a response-able state.

SUCCESS SECRET #93

Take action on things that matter to you.

Through these success secrets, you have learned about your interests, setting goals, and balancing your needs with others' needs. Now you must know how to take action.

I told you that my grandmother taught me about goal setting. I also mentioned that action is an integral part of goal setting. It isn't enough to just plan. You must also do it. Otherwise, nothing comes of your dreams and aspirations.

Take a moment to think about the things you really want to accomplish. Maybe you love baking and want to learn a new way to make cupcakes. Or perhaps you are worried about people in your community who are out of work. Set a few goals in those areas you'd like to do to share your gifts and talents and help. Then make an action plan detailing how you will achieve your goals. The "Tips for Taking Action" can help.

Parents Sound Off

Parents know the passion you often feel for the world. They see you struggle with world events and are compelled to help you when you want to save the planet. Check out the following quotes to see what parents think about

WORKSHEET
I'm Response-Able When . . .

Directions: Complete the sentence below. List everything that help you be more response-able.

I am response-able when . . .

- I am well rested.
- I am not stressed out.
- _____
  _____
  _____
  _____

- _____
  _____
  _____
  _____

- _____
  _____
  _____
  _____

- _____
  _____
  _____
  _____

- _____
  _____
  _____
  _____

Tips for Taking Action

Try these ways to take action on your goals and dreams:

- Commit to doing one thing every day.
- Maintain a daily calendar of the things you need to do.
- Be sure to add your action items to the calendar.
- If you get off track, don't sweat it. Just get back on track as soon as possible.
- When you find your motivation faltering, go back and think about why you want to take this action.
- Keep a picture of your goal or dream somewhere where you can see it regularly.
- Celebrate your small victories along the way. No step toward your goals is too small to acknowledge.

your gifts and the obligations you sometimes feel to help everyone. Ask your parents what they think about service and giving back to the community and the world.

- "(My twice-exceptional child) is so frustrated with the world right now. He just doesn't understand why people can't be nice to each other. He wants to do something to help, and I don't know how to support his efforts. I mean, he's only 8."—*Tashawn*
- "My daughter is scared about the world. She watches the news and then asks me a million questions. I tried to get her to stop, but finally I realized this is just something that is important to her. So now we talk about what she sees and discuss things we can do to help."—*Kellyanne*
- "Both of my children are into service projects. Last Christmas, they didn't want presents. Instead, they just wanted to give back to families in need and celebrate the season through charitable acts. It is almost a compulsion to give with them."—*Khan*
- "I love that my daughter cares about others, but I wonder if she cares too much. I mean, she seems to get really distressed by world events. She even gets overwhelmed by her friends' problems at times."—*Adam*
- "I have a very goal-directed child. Everything is about her goals, lists of things to do, and plans—many, many, plans. I suppose this is a

good thing, but sometimes I just wish she would relax and let life just happen."—*Jessica*

What Do You Think?

Sharing your gifts is something you may feel both compelled and obligated to do. Sometimes it is a daunting task. Other times it is just overwhelming. Take a moment to reflect on the following questions as you determine what a healthy balance between giving and self-care is for you. Come back to these questions anytime you are starting to feel out of balance with your need to share your gifts.

What community or world events are you most passionate about?

How can you share your gifts in these areas that you care about?

What is one way you can stay in balance and be response-able?

Chapter 12

THRIVING AS A UNICORN

You made it to the final chapter. You've learned all about the attributes of giftedness, how your emotions can overwhelm you, and why your perfectionism is both a blessing and a curse. You've gotten tips about friendships, navigating problems, and accepting your gifts. Now it is time to talk about living authentically, with purpose, and embracing your specific brand of giftedness.

The success secrets throughout this chapter are all about

> "Never think that because you're smart, you are a nerd. You are whoever you want to be."—*Katie, age 12*

understanding who you are, accepting yourself, and practicing a little mental wellness. We live in a complex world with many demands and expectations. It's easy to feel a bit lost, lonely, and unsure of yourself. When this happens, remember who you are and what's important to you. Review what you've

 DOI: 10.4324/9781003232575-17

learned throughout the book and embrace your strengths. You can navigate this complicated world and thrive!

I titled this chapter "Thriving as a Unicorn." To me, every gifted person is a unique creature, just like mythological unicorns. You may go through periods of your life where you'd rather be a zebra and just fit in with everyone. But that isn't your destiny. Embrace what it means to be you and realize that in the end, unicorns just want to be unicorns—unique and magical.

SUCCESS SECRET **#94**

You have nothing to prove to anyone.

Growing up can be hard. Really hard. This is particularly true when you feel like you have to constantly prove your gifts to everyone. Maybe you struggle in school, despite your giftedness. Or maybe you are in a class with people even brighter than you, so you feel like you can't measure up. Whatever the case may be, sometimes you get stuck feeling like you have to prove your giftedness.

> "You shouldn't have to 'prove' your giftedness to your friends or teachers."—*Christina, age 11*

The truth is that you don't have to prove who you are to anyone. You just have to be who you are. Stop trying to blend in, and stop worrying what everyone else is thinking. Go back to the hula hoop story and remember that the only things you have any control over are you and your thoughts and actions. You don't have control over what people choose to think about you, so stop stressing over it.

SUCCESS SECRET **#95**

Be true to yourself.

> "Never stop trying because you want to fit in with 'normal' kids."—*Madison, age 11*

Once you stop stressing over trying to prove your giftedness, you can focus on being true to you. How do you do this? The first step is to figure out all of the wonderful things that are true about you, as well as all of the wonderful things that sometimes get in your way. Figure out what it means to be you.

Sometimes you will like what you discover about yourself, and sometimes you will not. Remember that you can change how you react to things and even what you think about them, but you won't be able to change everything. How your body is built is largely due to biology that you can't change. The same is true with skin and eye color, medical conditions, and your giftedness.

Embrace everything about you, and you know what? Other people will, too.

SUCCESS SECRET #96

Never try to hide your giftedness—it won't work.

I want to share a little story with you about a girl I once knew. We'll call her Allison. Allison had a very hard time making friends at school. She was a very smart girl and not at all interested in the things other third graders cared about. Her classmates wanted to play with dolls, but Allison liked to play with chemistry sets. Her classmates liked to read fairy tales, but Allison read Shakespeare. And her classmates liked to dress up as princesses, but Allison liked to dress up as a doctor.

Allison did not fit in.

One day, Allison decided she would change and be more like her classmates.

> "My goal this year is to embrace my gifts instead of trying to keep them on the down low."—*Savana, age 14*

She stopped playing with chemistry sets, stopped reading Shakespeare, and stopped pretending to be a doctor. She tried to embrace everything her classmates liked to do.

What do you think happened? Did Allison make friends? Was she happy?

You're right . . . she was miserable. And although her classmates did accept her for a little while, Allison could not keep up the charade. Pretty soon she went back to her chemistry sets and Shakespeare. Allison learned that she couldn't change who she was on the inside to please other people. She could only figure out how to be herself.

The good news is that Allison eventually found other kids who understood her unique qualities.

Have you figured out how to embrace your many gifts? Or are you still hiding your giftedness just a little?

SUCCESS SECRET **#97**

Remember to take care of yourself.

Being a gifted kid is both great and difficult. But, regardless of whether you're having an easy time with your giftedness or a hard time, there are a few things you can do to manage your life better. The biggest thing is taking good care of yourself. No one copes well when they are tired, hungry, or stressed. Remembering to make yourself a priority in your life is essential to being successful now and later on. Check out the "Tips for Taking Care of Yourself."

SUCCESS SECRET **#98**

Step out of your comfort zone.

One of the best ways to resist stereotypes and labels is to step out of your comfort zone and broaden your experiences. If you like to read adventure books, try reading fantasy. If you like to play group sports like baseball, try a different type of sport like mountain biking. You don't have to like everything you try—that isn't the point. The point is to broaden your experiences in the world and try new things.

I'm going to challenge you a bit now: I want you to try one new thing every week for a month. It could be a trying a food you never thought you'd like or maybe reading a book that is different for you. It doesn't matter what it is you're trying; it only matters that you do something new each and every week. Check out the worksheet "New Things I'd Like to Try."

After a month or so, write down all of the new things you tried. How did you like them? Which ones would you want to try again?

Repeat this process a few times each year. Before you know it, you will have tried more new things than you ever thought possible.

Tips for Taking Care of Yourself

1. **Get plenty of rest.** Most kids your age require at least 8 hours every night. Developing a bedtime routine can help if you have a hard time getting to sleep at night.

2. **Eat healthy foods.** Junk food may taste good, but it can really work against your brain functioning and overall health. Learn about good food choices and commit to eating healthy every day.

3. **Stay active.** Exercise is an essential part of taking care of yourself. Most schools don't have daily P.E., so it is really important to spend a part of every day being active. Dance, jumping rope, playing ball—all of these forms of exercise will improve your brain functioning, keep you healthy, and make it easier to get to sleep at night. Not only that, but exercise is one of the best ways to combat stress.

4. **Relax.** We live in a very busy world. Learning to relax a little every day can help rejuvenate our minds and our bodies. Try deep breathing, yoga, prayer, or just sitting in silence for a few minutes every day.

5. **Play.** Life isn't just about work, especially when you're a kid. It is easy to get too busy with school and your extra activities to remember to play. But, playing is just as important as everything else. So find a way to carve out a few minutes of playtime. You can play with a friend, a pet, or your parents. Just a few minutes a day is all you need to stay in balance.

SUCCESS SECRET #99

Don't take yourself too seriously.

Sometimes friendships end prematurely—not because people move or interests change. Sometimes they end for much simpler reasons: You were too hard on yourself and your friendships, you wanted your friends to make you feel okay, or you expected too much from everyone.

Or you forgot to have a little fun.

Gifted kids naturally take things a little too seriously. Being a deep thinker means that your mind is constantly working and seeing the bigger,

WORKSHEET
New Things I'd Like to Try

1. List all of the things you would like to try one day. Be creative when making this list. Don't worry if it isn't realistic.

   _____

   _____

   _____

2. Go through the list and separate your ideas into the following categories:

   a. Things you can try within the next month:

   _____

   _____

   _____

   b. Things you can try in a year or so:

   _____

   _____

   _____

   c. Things you can try as an adult:

   _____

   _____

   _____

3. Focus on the things you can try within the next month or so. What would it take for you to try these? Do you have the ability to access these things?

   _____

   _____

   _____

4. Make a goal to try something new each week. Keep track of the things you accomplish.

5. Find a way to celebrate the new things you have tried each month. Be sure to update your lists as time goes by.

Trying new things is a great way to keep life interesting, not to mention a great way to discover new things about yourself.

harder things in life. Many times you expect big things from yourself, your family, and your friends. There is little room for error.

Relationships aren't like math problems in school: There are seldom single answers to things. People are messy and complicated. There is a way to deal with relationships better. First, stop taking yourself too seriously. Remember that people are flawed, like we discussed earlier. Lighten up—on yourself and your friends. Allow people to make mistakes. Allow yourself to do the same.

> "I wish I knew how to take it easy on myself and my friends when I was younger. It would've helped things—a lot." —Rosi, age 13

And laugh. Find the humor in life. It will smooth things out.

The more you can remember to relax and allow people to be exactly who they are on any given day, the easier it is to see and appreciate the amazing things they do.

SUCCESS SECRET #100

Know your story.

Every person has a unique story, a narrative of their life that caused them to be exactly where they are today. Sometimes the story is simple; often, it is more complicated. Regardless, knowing your story helps you understand who you are and why you do what you do.

This isn't to say that you *are* your story—you are not. You are actually the author of the story. If you don't like what has happened to date, write something new. This isn't always easy. Many of you may have barriers in opportunity and feel like a victim to your story or your circumstances. It is easy to see how this can be true in our world today. But I want you to remember that you have the ability to rewrite your story more than you may realize. Think of the hula hoop activity again. You are in control of what is inside that hula hoop.

When a lack of opportunity threatens you, use your gifts to see if there are positive ways to change the outcomes. The world is full of stories of people who faced impossible odds and wound up achieving their dreams. This can be you as well. It begins with knowing your story. Then decide how you will edit it.

Try to complete the worksheet "My Story."

WORKSHEET
My Story

Directions: Follow the steps below and write the important events of your story in the box provided.

1. Write down each major event from your life that you believe shaped you in some way. Remember, this is your origin story. A good story has a beginning, a middle, and an end. Your story does, too. Write it all down.

2. After you've written your story, reflect on the following:
    a. What does the story make you think about?
    b. What beliefs did you form about the world as a result of the experience?
    c. What lessons did you learn from your story?
    d. What strengths do you see within YOU in the story?
    e. How can you use these strengths to help you grow from your experiences?

Note. Adapted from Fonseca, 2020.

SUCCESS SECRET #101

Embrace your unique brand of giftedness.

As I stated at the beginning of this chapter, you are a unicorn—unique and magical. The attributes of giftedness you have are unique to you. Although it is great to see yourself as an individual being, it is also tough. Especially when you are a child. There is tremendous pressure to conform, fit in, belong. Although cultivating a strong sense of belonging is vital to our well-being, this doesn't mean we should strive to be just like everyone else.

Go through all of the personal development tasks throughout the book. Read what you have learned about yourself. Then make a poster celebrating your unique brand of giftedness (see the worksheet "To Be ME"). Be you. Be original. You will still find your group of other unicorns also learning to be originals. Together, you can celebrate each other's diversity and uniqueness.

Parents Sound Off

Parents know that growing up gifted is a challenge. They are proud of everything you are and everything you have become. They are worried that your intensities will get the better of you sooner or later. The following quotes reflect parents' thoughts about your unique qualities. Read over their words. Then talk with your parents and see what they think.

- "I love all of my child's little quirks. But sometimes I worry that she'll be bullied because of them."—*Becca*
- "All I really want for my son (who is both gifted and autistic) is for others to see how special and brilliant he is."—*Tang*
- "My gifted children are all very different from one another. Just when I think I know what it means to be gifted, one of them surprises me. I guess that is just what *normal* is for them."—*Natalie*
- "I tell my child to just be herself. I am not sure, though, if that is the right thing to say. It seems like she is really unhappy in her own skin."—*Leticia*
- "Sometimes I wonder if I should've just avoided the whole gifted label with my child. But I can't deny who he is—and honestly, I wouldn't want to."—*Jerad*

WORKSHEET
To Be ME

Directions: Review all of the activities you have done throughout the book. In the space below or on a separate sheet of paper, make a poster that shows all of your different characteristics, strengths and values. Add your life motto somewhere on the page. Be as creative as you'd like as you create something that represents your unique gifts and talents.

What Do You Think?

Living as a gifted child can be challenging. Sometimes you find people who understand you. Often, however, you may find yourself having to explain your giftedness to people. People may have expectations that feel intolerable. You may think you have to do everything in a certain way, or that being gifted means only one specific thing.

Take a moment to reflect on the following questions and see what giftedness means to you and ways you can live your best life.

What makes you unique?

Do you ever try to hide your giftedness? Why and when?

What quality or qualities of being gifted are most like you?

Final Thoughts

Facing life as a gifted kid can be a very unique experience. At times, it'll be a blast as you get to stretch that beautiful mind of yours, discovering new and sometimes surprising things. Other days you may wish you never were given the label of gifted. You'll be intense, frustrated, and emotional. You may get annoyed with school, your friends, and your parents. It may feel hard being gifted. You may even be tempted to try to *not* be smart anymore.

However, you know that won't work. Like it or not, you are a fantastic gifted kid!

I hope you find something in these pages to help you along this journey, something to remind you that you aren't alone as you work through your more intense nature, and something to make the job of growing up a little easier.

The success strategies, although simple, are not always easy to master. You may get frustrated as you attempt them—that's okay. Just go through and try the ones that you can. Revisit the book as things come up. What worked today may not work for you tomorrow.

To end things, I wanted to share some final thoughts from parents and kids just like you—their ideas about growing up gifted.

Parents Sound Off

Parents know that growing up is difficult regardless of labels or anything else. Being gifted just adds another layer to the experience—one that has benefits and drawbacks. The following quotes are their ideas about the world of giftedness and their children. Read over their thoughts, and then talk with your parents and see what they think about raising a gifted child.

- "I think my relationship with my gifted child comes from an understanding of what it was to be labeled gifted as a child myself and always feeling like I was swimming upstream."—*Kathleen*
- "The biggest part is to make sure they know they are accepted for who they are and are loved very much for everything they are."—*Thomas*
- "Being gifted doesn't mean my daughter is good at everything she tries—that is what I want people to realize."—*Nichole*
- "The hardest, and most important, part of parenting my gifted kid is knowing how to help him stay grounded without quashing his creativity or dreams. It has been a constant balancing act."—*Lu*
- "I am proud of my gifted son. But I worry that he may never get the opportunities he deserves, even though he is gifted. The world just doesn't always work that way."—*Dashon*

What Do You Think?

Before you reflect on your own final thoughts about growing up gifted, I want you to take a minute to read what some other kids just like you believe.

- "People need to know that being gifted means I'm intense sometimes—with school, with my friends, with everything. I'm not strange or crazy because I'm this way."—*Matwa, age 11*
- "Being gifted is awesome. Just embrace it. You can't really change it anyways."—*Ben, age 9*

- "Being in GATE means you have a lot of strengths, but don't forget you still have troubles—things you aren't good at. It's hard to remember that sometimes."—*Kimberly, age 10*
- "I'm in a gifted class at school. It's cool because people get me, but it's also really hard. Everyone is so smart. Now I feel like I'm left out—like I'm not as smart."—*Liam, age 9*
- "I wish my teachers understood that being gifted doesn't mean I'm good at everything. Not even close."—*Janice, age 12*

Most kids recognize that being identified as gifted is a good thing. However, they also know that people make assumptions about gifted kids and sometimes things can be very hard.

Now it's your turn. Take a moment to reflect on everything you have learned through the book and then answer the following questions.

Come back and look at the questions often. As you grow and change, so will your answers. The important thing to remember is that you are an amazing person. Embracing your giftedness, both the good parts and the not-so-good parts will make you even more amazing.

If you have some advice you'd like to share, or if there are additional tips you need, please reach out to me at christine@christinefonseca.com. I would love to hear from you.

—*Christine Fonseca*

Which Success Secret helped you the most? Why?

Which Success Secret gave you the most trouble? Why?

How do you feel about being gifted?

Recommended Resources for Parents and Kids

General Information on Giftedness

Information related to giftedness can sometimes be hard to find. Fortunately, there are a few fantastic websites that provide information on every topic imaginable related to giftedness, advocating for the gifted, and the most recent research in the field. Here are a few of my favorite and most-trusted websites:

1. National Association for Gifted Children (https://www.nagc.org): This is a great site for everything from advocacy efforts to the latest research in the field.

2. Supporting Emotional Needs of the Gifted (https://www.sengifted.org): This site includes great articles related to the social and emotional needs of gifted children. Also, it's a great source for information related to forming parent support groups.

3. Davidson Institute for Talent Development (https://www.davidson gifted.org): This is an excellent site for articles related to giftedness.
4. Hoagies' Gifted Education Page (https://www.hoagiesgifted.org): Hoagies' is a fantastic site for information about giftedness and links for parents and kids to explore.

Books for Gifted Kids

Growing up as a gifted kid can be challenging. For additional tips on dealing with emotional intensity, anxiety, or perfectionism, check out these great books:

1. *The Gifted Kids Workbook: Mindfulness Skills to Help Children Reduce Stress, Balance Emotions, and Build Confidence* by Heather Boorman (Instant Help, 2018): This is a great book to help gifted children begin to learn strategies to manage intensities and develop their emotional intelligence.
2. *Being You: A Girl's Guide to Mindfulness* by Catherine Hannay (Prufrock Press, 2019): This is a very useful guide to mindfulness activities.
3. *Nothing You Can't Do!: The Secret Power of Growth Mindsets* by Mary Cay Ricci (Prufrock Press, 2018): Got an underachiever? This book will help children discover how grit and perseverance, as well as a growth mindset, can make all the difference at school and in life.
4. *Letting Go: A Girl's Guide to Breaking Free of Stress and Anxiety* by Christine Fonseca (Prufrock Press, 2017). This book is for young women looking to tame the beast of stress and anxiety.
5. *Anxiety-Free Kids: An Interactive Guide for Parents and Children* (2nd ed.) by Bonnie Zucker (Prufrock Press, 2016): This is a terrific guide for children and parents dealing with anxiety.
6. *When Gifted Kids Don't Have All the Answers: How to Meet Their Social and Emotional Needs* (Rev. ed.) by James R. Delisle and Judy Galbraith (Free Spirit Publishing, 2016): This is good book geared for children and the problems they tend to face in the educational setting.
7. *What to Do When Good Isn't Good Enough: The Real Deal on Perfectionism: A Guide for Kids* by Thomas S. Greenspon (Free Spirit Publishing, 2007): This is good resource for younger children that provides lots of practical strategies.

References

Alias, A., Rahman, S., Majid, R. A., & Yassin, S. (2013). Dabrowski's over-excitabilities profile among gifted students. *Asian Social Science, 9*(16), 120–125.

Banner, V. (2008). *5 amazing breakthroughs discovered by accident.* https://www.qualityhealth.com/health-lifestyle-articles/5-amazing-breakthroughs-discovered-accident

Baumann, D., Ruch, W., Margelisch, K., Gander, F., & Wagner, L. (2019). Character strengths and life satisfaction in later life: An analysis of different living conditions. *Applied Research in Quality of Life, 15*, 329–347. https://doi.org/10.1007/s11482-018-9689-x

Clark, B. (2013). *Growing up gifted: Developing potential of children at home and at school* (8th ed.). Pearson.

Fonseca, C. (2013). *Quiet kids: Help your introverted child succeed in an extroverted world.* Prufrock Press.

Fonseca, C. (2016). *Emotional intensity in gifted students: Helping kids cope with explosive feelings* (2nd ed.). Prufrock Press.

Fonseca, C. (2017). *Letting go: A girl's guide to breaking free of stress and anxiety*. Prufrock Press.

Fonseca, C. (2019). *The caring child: Raising empathetic and emotionally intelligent children*. Prufrock Press.

Fonseca, C. (2020). *Healing the heart: Helping your child thrive after trauma*. Prufrock Press.

HowStuffWorks. (2007). *9 things invented or discovered by accident*. http://science.howstuffworks.com/innovation/9-things-invented-or-discovered-by-accident.htm

National Association for Gifted Children. (2019). *Definition of giftedness*. https://www.nagc.org/sites/default/files/Position%20Statement/Definition%20of%20Giftedness%20%282019%29.pdf

Niemiec, R. (2019). Six functions of character strengths for thriving at times of adversity and opportunity: A theoretical perspective. *Applied Research in Quality of Life, 15*, 551–572. https://doi.org/10.1007/s11482-018-9692-2

Prabhune, A. (2015). *10 inventions that changed the world, but were made by mistake*. https://www.storypick.com/inventions-made-by-mistake

Sinek, S. (2009). *Start with why: How great leaders inspire everyone to take action*. Penguin Books.

Sword, L. (2006a). *Psycho-social needs: Understanding the emotional, intellectual and social uniqueness of growing up gifted*. http://talentdevelop.com/articles/PsychosocNeeds.html

Sword, L. (2006b). *The gifted introvert*. http://highability.org/the-gifted-introvert

Tetreault, N., Hasse, J., & Duncan, S. (2016). *The gifted brain*. Gifted Research and Outreach.

Webb, J. T., Gore, J. L., Amend, E. R., & DeVries, A. R. (2007). *A parent's guide to gifted children*. Great Potential Press.

About the Author

Christine Fonseca is a licensed educational psychologist, critically acclaimed author, and a nationally recognized speaker on topics related to educational psychology, mental health, giftedness, and using storytelling to heal past wounds. She provides professional learning and enrichment opportunities for students and educators across the United States.

Using her experience consulting and coaching educators and parents, Christine brings her expertise to *Psychology Today*, authoring the parenting blog *Parenting for a New Generation*. She has written self-help articles for Parents.com, Johnson & Johnson, and *Justine Magazine*. Her appearance on the popular gifted education podcast Mind Matters was one of its most downloaded episodes.

Christine uses her fictional stories to explore the more complex aspects of humanity through young adult and adult thrillers, urban fantasies, and contemporary stories. As a trauma-impacted survivor, Christine believes in the power of storytelling as a key to healing past wounds. She delivers soul-centered writing workshops designed to help writers get into touch with their authentic voice and bring that to both nonfiction and fiction writing.

Christine's critically acclaimed titles include *Emotional Intensity in Gifted Students, Raising the Shy Child* and *Letting Go: A Girl's Guide to Breaking Free of Stress and Anxiety*.

Christine lives in Southern California with her husband and children.

Printed in the United States
by Baker & Taylor Publisher Services